a DAILY INVITATION *to*
FRIENDSHIP *with* GOD

DESTINY IMAGE BOOKS BY BILL JOHNSON

Hosting the Presence

Hosting the Presence Every Day

When Heaven Invades Earth

The Supernatural Power of the Transformed Mind

Strengthen Yourself in the Lord

Releasing the Spirit of Prophecy

Dreaming with God

Here Comes Heaven

Release the Power of Jesus

The Supernatural Ways of Royalty

Spiritual Java

A Life of Miracles

Center of the Universe

Dream Journal

a DAILY INVITATION *to*

FRIENDSHIP *with* GOD

Dreaming with God to TRANSFORM *your* WORLD

Inspiring Quotes, Thoughts, and Reflections from

BILL JOHNSON

Material adapted from previously published work, *Dreaming With God*.

DESTINY IMAGE® PUBLISHERS, INC.
P.O. Box 310, Shippensburg, PA 17257-0310
"Promoting Inspired Lives."

This book and all other Destiny Image and Destiny Image Fiction books are available at Christian bookstores and distributors worldwide.

Cover design by Eileen Rockwell

For more information on foreign distributors, call 717-532-3040.
Reach us on the Internet: www.destinyimage.com.

ISBN 13 TP: 978-0-7684-0954-3
ISBN 13 eBook: 978-0-7684-0955-0

For Worldwide Distribution, Printed in the U.S.A.
1 2 3 4 5 6 7 8 / 20 19 18 17 16

Contents

Introduction

By Bill Johnson

One of the most remarkable discoveries in my life is that God wants to co-labor with me. While I am thrilled with the concept, I've never been able to grasp the reason why. Everything He's called me to do, He can do better—infinitely better. It's become apparent that He did not choose me for what I can do for Him. He chose me because He loves me. Period. The reality of co-laboring has also invaded my dream life, meaning He has interest in my desires. While I'm sure this includes the dreams in our sleep, it's my life's dreams that He seems to like. Why else would He repeat His statement, "Whatever you desire, I will give to you"?

Jesus gave this "blank check" to His disciples four different times in John 14–16. Each time, He invited them to dream. I don't think He was inviting them, and now us, into dreaming about building our own empires or creating some acceptable form of a self-centered gospel. But He was inviting us to dream just the same. When James and John wanted to call down fire on the Samaritans in Luke 9, Jesus said no, rebuking them for such corrupt desires. I guess it might seem like a contradiction to some for Jesus to invite them to bring any desire to Him, and then have Him say no to their request. It'll help us when we realize that God always reserves the right to deny any request that undermines our purpose.

The Scriptures tell us to *"seek first the kingdom of God...and all these things will be added to us."* I think *all these things* are what we dream about. *The kingdom of God* is what He dreams about. It seems to be consistent with the implications of this verse to say, *If we dream His dreams, He'll dream ours.*

Proverbs 13:12b says, *"Desire fulfilled is a tree of life."* The Tree of Life connects us to our eternal purpose, which basically means we were created to co-labor with God, seeing dreams and desires fulfilled. The fulfillment of dreams is, in part, our reason for being. God is looking for the God-like dreams from His people shaping the course of history on planet earth. This is our privilege.

I believe that the daily readings in *A Daily Invitation to Friendship with God* will help to connect the reader to his or her eternal purpose of bearing the fruit of answered prayers—fulfilled dreams. By this process of co-laboring, God is delighted and glorified.

Blessings!

BILL JOHNSON

Part One

CO-LABORING WITH GOD

God has made Himself vulnerable to the desires of His people.

1

APPREHENDED BY GOD

The disciples lived in awe of this One who called them to leave everything and follow.

It was an easy choice. When He spoke, something came alive in them that they never knew existed. There was something in His voice that was worth living for—worth giving one's life for.

Every day with Jesus was filled with a constant barrage of things they could not understand; whether it was a demoniac falling at Jesus' feet in worship, or the overbearing religious leaders becoming silent in His presence; it was all overwhelming. Their lives had taken on a meaning and purpose that made everything else disappointing at best. Oh, they had their personal issues, for sure, but they had been apprehended by God and now nothing else mattered.

2

THE ULTIMATE PROMOTION

"No longer do I call you servants, for a servant does not know what his master is doing; but I have called you friends, for all things that I heard from My Father I have made known to you."
—JOHN 15:15

Toward the end of His earthly life, Jesus gave His disciples the ultimate promotion. He told the twelve that He no longer called them servants, but friends. To be in the same room with Him, or even to admire Him from a distance, was more than they could have asked for. But Jesus brought them into His life. They had proven themselves worthy of the greatest promotion ever experienced by humanity—from servants to intimates.

3

FOCUS OF FRIENDSHIP

When Jesus gave His disciples this promotion (from servants to intimates), He did so by describing the difference between the two positions. Servants don't know what their master is doing. They don't have access to the personal, intimate realm of their master. They are task-oriented. Obedience is their primary focus—and rightly so, for their lives depend on success in that area. But friends have a different focus. It almost sounds blasphemous to say that obedience is not the top concern for the friend, but it is true.

Obedience will always be important, as John 15:14 highlights, *"You are my friends if you do whatever I command you."* But friends are less concerned about disobeying than they are about disappointing. The disciples' focus shifted from the commandments to the presence, from the assignment to the relationship, from "what I do for Him" to "how my choices affect Him."

4

FRIENDSHIP GRANTS ACCESS TO NEW KNOWLEDGE

As we embrace the promotion to friendship with God, *what we know changes* as we gain access to the heart of the Father. His heart is the greatest resource of information we need to function successfully in all of life. Jesus paid the price of our access to the Father, thereby granting us the *freedom* that comes from the truth we gain through that unlimited knowledge of His heart. Liberty is found in this phase of the promotion.

5

FRIENDSHIP OPENS DOORS FOR NEW ENCOUNTERS

When we receive access to friendship with God, our *experience* changes. Encounters with God as an intimate are quite different from those of a servant. His heartbeat becomes our heartbeat as we celebrate the shift in our own desires. The realm of His presence becomes our greatest inheritance, and divine encounters our greatest memories. Personal transformation is the only possible result from these supernatural experiences.

6

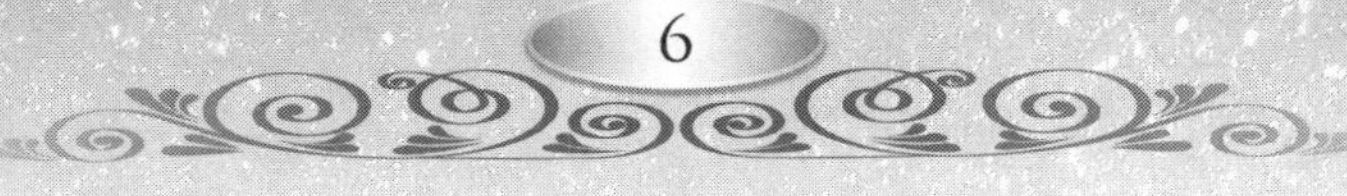

Friendship Determines Identity

Our identity sets the tone for all we do and become.

Christians who live out of who they really are cannot be crippled by the opinions of others.

They don't work to fit into other people's expectations, but burn with the realization of who the Father says they are.

7

ENJOY THE FAVOR OF YOUR FRIEND

Mary sought to please Jesus by being with Him while Martha tried to please Him through service. When Martha became jealous, she asked Jesus to tell Mary to help in the kitchen. Most servants want to degrade the role of the friend to feel justified in their works-oriented approach to God. Jesus' response is important to remember: *"Mary has chosen the better part"* (see John 10:42).

Martha was making sandwiches that Jesus never ordered.

Doing more for God is the method servants use to increase in favor. A friend has a different focus entirely. They enjoy the favor they have and use it to spend time with their friend.

8

Working from Presence

To say we need both Marys and Marthas is to miss the point entirely. And it simply isn't true. I've heard it said that nothing would ever get done if we didn't have Marthas. That, too, is a lie. That teaching comes mostly from servants who are intimidated by the lifestyle of friends. Mary wasn't a non-worker; she just learned to serve from His presence, only making the sandwiches that Jesus ordered.

Working from His presence is better than working for His presence.

9

INVITED INTO GOD'S COUNSEL

When God was going to destroy Israel, He told Moses to get out of the way because He was going to kill the people Moses had led out of Egypt into the wilderness. Moses then reminded God that they weren't his people—they were God's, and not only that, he didn't lead them out of Egypt, God did! God responded by basically acknowledging he was right, and then He promised not to kill them. The astonishing thing isn't so much that God changed His mind and spared Israel; rather, it was that He expected Moses to come into the counsel of His will, and Moses knew it.

10

Participation in Heaven's Process

Moses, Abraham, and other covenant friends throughout history all seemed to have a common awareness of God's expectation that they be involved in the demonstration of His will, influencing the outcome of a matter. They understood that the responsibility rested on their shoulders, and they must act before God to get what people needed. The priestly role of an intercessor was never more clearly illustrated. The primary focus of God's will wasn't whether or not to destroy Israel; it was to bring Moses in on the process. His will is not always focused on events; it is focused on His friends drawing near into His presence, standing in their roles as delegated ones.

The will of God is as much process as it is outcome—often fluid, not static.

11

Blank Checks from Jesus

As kids, many of us dreamed about being granted one wish. Solomon got the "one wish." When God appeared to Solomon and gave him that opportunity, it forever raised the bar of our expectations in prayer. The disciples were given the same "wish," only better. Instead of one blank check, they were given an unlimited supply of blank checks. And this gift was specifically granted in the context of their friendship with God.

Surrounding their promotion to friendship, Jesus gave His disciples this amazing list of promises. Each promise was a blank check they were to live by and use throughout their lives for the expansion of the Kingdom.

12

God never intended that the believer be a puppet on a string. God actually makes Himself vulnerable to the desires of His people. In fact, it can be said,

> **"If it matters to you, it matters to Him."**

While much of the Church is waiting for the next word from God, He is waiting to hear the dreams of His people.

He longs for us to take our role, not because He needs us, but because He loves us.

14

Discovering the Pleasures of God

There is no question that spending time with God changes our desires. We always become like the One we worship. But it's not because we've been programmed to wish for the things He wants us to wish for; it's because in friendship we discover the things that please Him—the secret things of His heart.

15

A LONGING TO PLEASE THE FATHER

It is the instinct of the true believer to search for and find that which brings pleasure to the Father. Our nature actually changes at conversion. It is our new nature to seek to know God and to please Him with our thoughts, ambitions, and desires.

16

The Offspring of Fellowship

If I take time to ponder an offense I experienced some years ago, and I begin to wonder if God ever judged that person, the desires of vindication and retaliation will stir up in my heart. Why? Because I have been fellowshipping with the *father* of bitterness, and those desires are the *children* formed in my heart. If fellowshipping with evil can produce evil desires in us, how much more should it be said that time with God forms desires in us that have eternity in mind and ultimately bring Him glory? The thing to note is this: These desires are not there by command; they are in our hearts because of our fellowship with God. They are the offspring of our relationship with Him.

17

DON'T OVERSHOOT GOD'S WILL

Many believers discount their desires, automatically trying to get rid of everything they want in order to prove their surrender to God. Their selfless approach overshoots the will of God and actually denies the fact that God is the Father of the dreams and abilities within them. It sounds good on the outside because of its selfless religious appeal, but it works against God's purposes on the inside.

18

LIFE INSIDE THE KINGDOM

Most believers still don't see the difference between the entrance *to the* Kingdom and life *in the* Kingdom. We enter on a straight and narrow road, saying, *"Not my will but Yours be done."* The only door is Christ Jesus. The only way to find life in Christ is to come in complete abandonment to Him.

But life in the Kingdom, which is past the narrow entrance of salvation, is completely different. It's bigger on the inside than it is on the outside. It is here we find the Lord saying to us that we're no longer servants, but friends.

Just as the Cross precedes the resurrection, so our abandonment to His will precedes God attending to ours.

But the opposite emphasis also has dangers—if we never become people of desire, we will never accurately and effectively represent Christ on the earth.

20

"...desire fulfilled is a tree of life."
—Proverbs 13:12 NASB

Solomon's words revisit the subject of the tree of life found in Genesis. It connected Adam and Eve to eternity.

Here we are told that a believer will experience the tree of life as their desires are fulfilled. This implies that those who taste the wonder of fulfilled desires in Christ will be given eternal perspective and identity through that fulfillment. The process of surrender, personal transformation, and fulfilled desires is the training ground for reigning with Christ forever.

21

THE JOY OF ANSWERED PRAYER

In John 16:24, it says that God wants to answer our desires (prayers), "*that your joy may be full.*" No wonder there's been so little joy in the Church.

Joy is the result of our redeemed heart reveling in its participation in God's unfolding plan for the earth through prayer. More specifically, joy comes through having our prayers answered.

22

YOUR INVITATION TO EXTREME JOY

Answered prayers, especially those that require supernatural intervention, make us happy! And happy people are fun to be with. Perhaps that's why Jesus was called the friend of sinners (see Luke 7:34). His joy exceeded all those around Him. Moment by moment, day after day, He saw His prayers answered by His heavenly Father.

His joy was what many would consider extreme. In Luke 10:21, it says, *"Jesus rejoiced in the Spirit."* The word *rejoiced* in that context suggests "shouting and leaping with joy." Even proximity to Jesus brought joy. John the Baptist leapt for joy in his mother's womb because Mary, who was pregnant with Jesus, entered the room. Jesus' joy is contagious and must become the mark of true believers once again.

23

DREAMERS WHO WRITE HISTORY

"Blessed be the Lord God of Israel, who spoke with His mouth to my father David, and with His hand has fulfilled it, saying, 'Since the day that I brought My people Israel out of Egypt, I have chosen no city from any tribe of Israel in which to build a house, that My name might be there; but I chose David to be over My people Israel.' Now it was in the heart of my father David to build a temple for the name of the Lord God of Israel."
—1 KINGS 8:15-17

God said that He didn't choose a city, He chose a man, and the idea for a temple was in the heart of the man. God basically said, "The temple wasn't my idea. David was my idea." Incredible!

David's creativity and desires helped write history because God embraced them. David gave us many Kingdom principles, which set the direction in which we are to live. It is as if he said, "Dreamers! Come! Let's dream together and write the story of human history."

24

You are God's idea, and He longs to see the treasure that is in your heart. As we learn to dream with God we become co-laborers with Him.

25

DEFINING THE NATURE OF YOUR WORLD

God assigned Adam the task of naming all the animals (see Gen. 2:19). Names had much richer meaning in those days because they represented the nature of something. I believe that Adam was actually assigning to each animal its nature, its realm of authority, and the dimension of glory it would enjoy. In reality, Adam's assignment was to help define the nature of the world he was to live in.

This co-laboring role was a creative role, complementary to God the Creator. God brings us into these situations, not because He can't do it Himself. He delights in seeing all that He made come into its identity in Him by embracing its divine purpose.

To embrace the privilege of creative expression is consistent with being made in the image and likeness of our Creator.

26

Desires Birthed in the Presence

"Therefore I say unto you, what things soever ye desire, when ye pray, believe that ye receive them, and ye shall have them."
—Mark 11:24 KJV

We are to pay attention to our desires while we're enjoying the presence of God in prayer.

Something happens in our time of communion with Him that brings life to our capacity to dream and desire. Our minds become renewed through divine encounter, making the perfect canvas for Him to paint on. We become co-laborers with Him in the master plan for planet earth.

27

RELEASED TO DREAM

Our dreams are not independent from God, but instead exist *because of God.* He lays out the agenda—*On earth as it is in Heaven*—and then releases us to run with it and make it happen!

As we grow in intimacy with Him, more of what happens in life is a result of our desires, not simply receiving and obeying specific commands from Heaven. God loves to build on our wishes and desires.

Part Two

THE CREATIVE EDGE

When unbelievers lead the way in inventions and artistic expression, it is because the Church has embraced a false kind of spirituality.

BORN TO DREAM

One of the most natural parts of being created in the image of God is the ability to dream.

It's a God-given gift. Yet many believers, in their attempts to please God, kill the very capacity He gave them. They reason, "To really please God I must get rid of everything to do with self!" It sounds spiritual to many, but it's more Buddhist than Christian. If we pursue that line of thinking for long we end up with neutered believers. Self-mutilation need not be physical to be a perversion.

Anytime we try to cut away at what God placed in us, we are entering a form of spirituality that the Scriptures do not support and are contributing to a spirit that works against us having a truly effective witness.

29

It is not wise to crucify the resurrected man and call it discipleship. The Cross is not for the new man; it's for the old man.

30

Many have even prayed, "None of me, all of You." God had none of us before we were born and didn't like it.

He created us for His pleasure.

A better prayer would be, "All of me covered by all of You!"

31

Is It Kingdom to Decrease?

John the Baptist's statement, "He must increase but I must decrease," is often misapplied in order to endorse the self-depreciating form of Christianity. Look at the context; he was passing the baton to Jesus.

John's job was to prepare the way for the Messiah. It was important for him to be out of the way as he closed out the Old Testament prophetic ministry. Jesus would bring about the fulfillment of all the prophets had announced and initiate God's manifest dominion on the planet. John the Baptist passed the baton to Jesus, who has passed it on to us *that we might increase.*

32

BOTH SIDES OF THE EQUATION

This confusion over our value and identity is sometimes most acute in revival, as the outpouring of the Spirit always brings an increased awareness of our sinfulness. Some of the greatest hymns of confession and contrition have been written during such seasons.

But the revelation of our sin and unworthiness is only half of the equation. Most revivals don't get past this one point, and therefore cannot sustain a move of God until it becomes a lifestyle. It's difficult to build something substantial on a negative.

The other half of the equation is how *holy* He is on our behalf and who we are as a result. When this is realized, our identity changes as we embrace the purpose of our salvation by faith. At some point we must go beyond being simply "sinners saved by grace."

As we learn to live from our position in Christ, we will bring forth the greatest exploits of all time.

33

STRIPPED-DOWN CHRISTIANITY

Throughout much of church history, people have been stripped of their God-given gifts, talents, and desires under the guise of *devotion to Christ.* This stripped-down version of Christianity removes the believer from ministry and relegates that privilege to a certain class of Christian called "ministers." The regular believer's role is reduced to financial and emotional support of those in public ministry. To work without fulfilled dreams and desires is to partner with the religious spirit that exalts routine without purpose and calls it suffering.

The honor of giving to promote ministry must not be devalued, but its emphasis should never be at the expense of each individual carrying their own creative expression of the Gospel through realizing their God-given dreams and desires.

Our heavenly Father is the Creator of all and the Giver of all good gifts. His children should bear His likeness, which means they should be creative.

When unbelievers lead the way in inventions and artistic expressions, it is because the Church has embraced a false kind of spirituality.

35

SOLUTION-MINDED

The renewed mind understands that the King's dominion must be realized in all levels of society for an effective witness to take place. Someone with a Kingdom mindset looks to the overwhelming needs of the world and says, "God has a solution for this problem. And I have legal access to His realm of mystery. Therefore I will seek Him for the answer!"

With a Kingdom perspective, we become the answer in much the same way Joseph and Daniel were to the kings of their day.

36

THE PRICE OF GOD'S DREAM

Learning the dreams of God for this world is our beginning place.

Dreaming can be expensive.

We know that the Father's dream of redeeming humanity cost Him the life of His Son. However, partnering with Him in His dreams will release in us a new capacity to dream like Him.

37

TOOLS FOR THE ASSIGNMENT

Wisdom and creativity must not be separated in the mind of the believer. They are the essential tools needed to complete our assignment of being an effective witness to the lost. It is wisdom that makes our role in this world desirable to them.

While most Christians have a value for wisdom, most do not have an equal value for the role of creativity in their God-given responsibilities. Yet it is creativity that illustrates the presence of wisdom: *"Wisdom is vindicated by all her children"* (Luke 7:35 NASB).

38

WISDOM, THE MASTER CRAFTSMAN

The first mention of a person filled with the Holy Spirit in Scripture was Bezalel. He was called upon to head up a building project for Moses. His assignment was to build God a house that He might dwell among His people. God revealed what He wanted that house to look like, but it would take a special gift of wisdom to know "how" to get it done.

That is where Bezalel came into the picture. He was given supernatural wisdom to complete the task with artistic excellence. It was wisdom that qualified him to take on this assignment, and it was wisdom that enabled him as an artisan or master craftsman to design and build what was in God's heart.

39

UNLOCKING THE POWER OF CREATIVITY

When creativity is the normal expression of God's people there is something that happens to all who oppose Him. They become disheartened.

The devil himself has no creative abilities whatsoever. All he can do is distort and deform what God has made. God is made known through His works. When His works flow through His children, their identity is revealed, and there is an inescapable revelation of the nature of God in the land. He is irresistible to those who have eyes to see.

40

WISDOM THAT CATCHES ATTENTION

Craftsmen are not simply woodworkers and painters. Nor does that title belong only to actors and musicians. Everyone doing their God-given task with *excellence, creativity, and integrity is a craftsman in the biblical sense.*

Schoolteachers, businessmen and women, doctors and lawyers, and all those who have surrendered their gifts to the purposes of God need to display divine wisdom. The opposition that surrounds us seems great, but it cannot stand against the demonstration of God's people wielding this great weapon of war.

From the housewife to the brain surgeon, from the preacher to the professor, all must be filled with the Spirit of God until we are known for wisdom, turning the heads of the *queens of Sheba once again* (see 1 Kings 10:1-10).

41

A Biblical Expression of Wisdom

The world's definition of wisdom is focused on the attainment and use of knowledge. It's not wrong; it's just misleading. The Church has adopted their incomplete definition, pursuing a wisdom that has no soul.

Biblical wisdom sees with divine perspective and is the creative expression of God, bringing practical solutions to the issues of everyday life.

Besides Jesus, Solomon was the wisest man to ever live. He caught the attention of his entire generation. People were in awe of his gift. The royalty in other nations envied his servants who had the privilege of being exposed to his gift on a daily basis.

A servant in the presence of wisdom is better off than a king without wisdom.

43

WHEN WISDOM DEFINES THE CHURCH AGAIN

The wisdom of God will again be reflected in His people. The Church, which is presently despised, will again be reverenced and admired. The Church will again be a *praise in the earth* (see Jer. 33:9).

The manifestations of wisdom are varied. Its nature can be seen in three words—integrity, creativity, and excellence.

Divine wisdom springs from integrity and becomes manifest through creative expression with excellence as its standard.

Wherever we find ourselves operating in any of these three expressions we are being touched by divine wisdom.

44

THE HOLINESS OF INTEGRITY

Integrity is the expression of God's character revealed in us, and that character is the beauty of His perfection—His holiness.

Holiness is the essence of His nature. It is not something He does or doesn't do. It is who He is. It is the same for us. We are holy because the nature of God is in us. It begins with a heart separated unto God and becomes evident in the Christ-nature expressed through us.

45

It is a shame for the Church to fall into the rut of predictability and call it "tradition." We must reveal who our Father is through creative expression.

46

We do not become culturally relevant when we become like the culture, but rather when we model what the culture hungers to become.

47

Embracing the Winds of Change

The Church is often guilty of avoiding creativity because it requires change. Resistance to change in reality is a resistance to the nature of God.

The statement *"For I, the Lord, do not change"* (Mal. 3:6 NASB) refers to His nature, which is perfect and unchanging. Yet He is always doing a new thing. As the winds of change blow, it will be easy to distinguish between those who are satisfied and those who are hungry. Change brings the secrets of the heart to light.

48

Excellence is the high standard set for personal achievement because of who we are in God and who God is in us. It is not the same as perfectionism.

Perfectionism is the cruel counterfeit of excellence, which flows from a religious spirit.

49

AWAKENING THE ARTISTS

Every five-year-old is an artist. It's an expression of their bent to create. But something happens when they enter grade school. Many educational systems narrow the definition of creativity to include only those who can draw or paint. By the time children are around ten years of age very few of them are still considered to be artists because of that narrow definition.

Today's Kingdom-oriented teachers must embrace the value of true wisdom and develop children's creative skills outside the traditional box called "art." It is divine wisdom displayed in creativity that brings an individual to the forefront in his or her field of influence.

50

AWE-INSPIRING WISDOM

It is wisdom that can take something that is an everyday item or concept and build upon it, creating something new and better. This is exactly what Solomon did. All kings of the day had cupbearers, servants, banqueting tables, and nice clothing for their servants. But there was something about his use of wisdom for everyday life that made him stand out above the rest. The queen of Sheba became speechless in response to Solomon's wisdom.

It's time for the Church to display a wisdom that causes the world to become silent again.

51

There is a misconception that often exists in the artistic community; creativity must come from pain. There's no question that some of the greatest works of art came from people who were troubled with life or experienced some of the worst tragedies. The reality is this—it often takes trauma to launch a person into a place of seeing the true priorities for life.

To embrace the privilege of creative expression is consistent with being made in the image and likeness of our Creator.

52

REVEALING THE MANIFOLD WISDOM OF GOD

"...that now the manifold wisdom of God might be made known by the church to the principalities and powers in the heavenly places, according to the eternal purpose which He accomplished in Christ Jesus our Lord."
—EPHESIANS 3:10-11

The Church has a clear assignment: We are to exhibit the multifaceted wisdom of God, *now*! It must permeate all we are and do. This neglected element is at the heart of our call to disciple nations. It is a part of the "witness" that turns people's heads in the same way as the nations were impacted by Solomon's wisdom. The spirit realm is watching and, more importantly, is affected by such a display. They must be reminded of their defeat, our victory, and the Father's eternal plan for the redeemed.

53

Mirroring Heaven on Earth

It's our connection to wisdom that clearly manifests our eternal purpose of reigning with Christ. When we walk in wisdom, we mirror the reality of Heaven here on earth and actually give Heaven a target for invasion.

In the same way, agreement with the devil empowers him to kill, steal, and destroy, so agreement with God releases God to accomplish His purposes in and through us to the world around us.

54

A Message to Experience

A reformation has begun. And at the heart of this great move of the Spirit is the total transformation of the people of God as they discover their true identity and purpose. Great purpose elicits great sacrifice.

Up until this time, many of our agendas have failed. Our attempts to make the Gospel palatable have had a serious effect on the world around us. The world has longed for a message they could *experience.* Yet many believers have simply tried to make the good news more intellectually appealing. This must stop! The natural mind cannot receive the things of the Spirit of God (see 1 Cor. 2:14).

The wisdom of God is foolishness to men. It's time to be willing to appear foolish again, that we might provide the world with a message of power that delivers, transforms, and heals. This is true wisdom. It alone satisfies the cry of the human heart.

55

Accessing Heaven's Revelation

There are melodies that have never been heard by the human ear that would bring people to their knees in surrender to Jesus. Musicians must hear the musical sounds of Heaven and reproduce them here.

There are medical secrets that are only one prayer away from revolutionizing the way people live.

Businesses strive day after day for success when the gift of wisdom can launch them into profound places of influence in a community.

Politicians look to consultants on how best to run a campaign. Yet there is wisdom in God that is so fresh and new that it will give them great favor with their constituents.

There are methods of education that have been hidden in the realms of God's mysteries.

He simply waits for one of His own to ask for the revelation. The list of heavenly answers is limitless. He looks for those who will ask.

56

When people pursue dreams but fail to see them fulfilled, they prepare the way for others who carry the same dream to eventually get the breakthrough that they were seeking. It is hard for many to take comfort in this thought, but that's because we usually think *it's all about us.*

There is no failure in faith.

57

Loss: A Seed for Breakthrough

Often a tragic loss here on earth is viewed quite differently in Heaven. What is honored in Heaven is frequently pitied or mocked here on earth. When a person dies while trying to live out an expression of faith, people often criticize the foolishness of their decision.

Few realize that their loss became the soil in which someone else could eventually realize their dream, because their loss actually paved the way to a breakthrough.

58

SETTING THE STAGE FOR A KING

Countless times throughout history there have been those who never realized a fulfillment of their dreams. Many come to the end of their lives with the overwhelming conclusion that they failed.

To our detriment, we have lived without the consciousness that a failed attempt at a dream often becomes the foundation of another person's success. Some water, others plant, and still others harvest. We all have an important role to set the stage for the King of kings to receive more glory. It's all about Him, not us.

59

All Authority

Demons aren't being made anymore. There's the same number wandering around the planet today as there were in Jesus' day, yet the population of people has increased into the billions, with believers numbering in the hundreds of millions.

On top of that, we all know from Scripture that there are two angels for every demon. And Jesus has *all* authority, so that leaves none for the devil. The *"all"* that Jesus possesses has been handed over to us.

His great plan is not designed so He will have to come and rescue us from the devil. It's the gates of hell that *will not* prevail against the advancing church (see Matt. 16:18). Jesus' authority has been given to us to do great exploits.

Part Three

The Value of Mystery

God hides things for us, not from us.

If I understand all that is going on in my Christian life, I have an inferior Christian life.

The walk of faith is to live according to the revelation we have received in the midst of the mysteries we can't explain. That's why Christianity is called *the faith.*

61

A True Cross-walk

All too often believers abandon or dilute their call in order to feel better about the things they cannot explain. To allow what we cannot answer to downgrade what God has shown us is to be carnal-minded.

Too many only obey what they understand, thus subjecting God to their judgments. God is not on trial; we are. A true *Cross-walk* is obeying where we have revelation in spite of the apparent contradiction in what we cannot explain.

To obey only when we see that there will be a favorable outcome is not obedience.

Obedience is supposed to be expensive.

63

Believing in a Culture of Unbelief

To embrace what God has shown us and to obey what He has commanded us, often in the midst of unanswerable questions, is an honor beyond measure. It is a great privilege to be a believing believer in the midst of a culture of unbelief. We must embrace this privilege.

No Christian should be unmoved by the Lord's question, "When I return, will I find faith on the earth?" I have set my heart to be His pleasure by living in faith.

64

DON'T LIMIT GOD

To have questions is healthy; to hold God hostage to those questions is not.

It sometimes creates an atmosphere that fulfills its own prophecy about the power of God not being for today. It shuts down the very anointing that would teach them otherwise.

65

Embracing Mystery

Not understanding is OK.

Restricting our spiritual life to what we understand is not.

It is immaturity at best. Such a controlling spirit is destructive to the development of a Christlike nature. God responds to faith but will not surrender to our demands for control. Maturity requires a heartfelt embrace of what we do not understand as an essential expression of faith.

66

A person's heart is more clearly seen by what they're willing to embrace without offense than by their expression of faith only in what they already understand.

67

Discipled Through Divine Encounter

The mind is trained through the experience of divine encounters and supernatural experiences initiated through the revelations from Scripture.

Revelation that doesn't lead to a divine encounter will only make us more religious, teaching us to embrace external standards without the internal realities.

68

Only what goes beyond my understanding is positioned to renew my mind.

"And the peace of God,
which surpasses all comprehension,
will guard your hearts and your
minds in Christ Jesus."
—Philippians 4:7 NASB

69

Belief Leads to Understanding

Our hearts can embrace things that our heads can't.

Our hearts will lead us where our logic would never dare to go.

No one ever attributes the traits of courage and valor to the intellect or the strength of human reasoning. Courage rises up from within and gives influence over the mind. In the same way, true faith affects the mind. Faith does not come from our understanding. It comes from the heart.

We do not believe because we understand; we understand because we believe.

"And without faith it is impossible to please Him, for he who comes to God must believe that He is and that He is a rewarder of those who seek Him."
—Hebrews 11:6 NASB

70

We'll know when our mind is truly renewed because the impossible will look logical.

71

Obeying Without Understanding

What we don't understand is sometimes as important as what we do. It's one thing to obey when God has given us understanding about a matter and quite another to obey while facing questions and circumstances that seem to contradict what we understand. So many fail at this point and then bring the Bible down to their level of experience.

Many do this to feel better about the fact that they are living in compromise—a compromise of their revelation from Scripture. Our challenge is instead to bring our lifestyle up to the standard of God's Word.

To embrace revelation with one hand and embrace mystery with the other forms a perfect cross. This is a cross that everyone who is hungry to do the works of Jesus will have to carry.

God must violate our logic to invite us away from the deception of relying on our own reasoning.

73

"It is the glory of God to conceal a matter, but the glory of kings is to search out a matter."
—Proverbs 25:2

People wonder why God doesn't always speak in more open terms—audibly, with visible signs, and other such ways. I don't know how or why it works this way, but the Bible indicates that *God receives more glory when He conceals*, rather than making things obvious.

It is more glorious for Him to hide and have us seek.

74

It is the mercy of God to withhold revelation from those who have no hunger for truth, because if they don't hunger for it, the chances are they won't obey it when they hear it.

75

God Conceals Revelation for Us

Revelation always brings responsibility, and hunger is the thing that prepares our hearts to carry the weight of that responsibility.

By keeping revelation from those without hunger, God actually protects them from certain failure to carry the responsibility it would lay on them. And so He conceals. Yet, He doesn't conceal *from us;* He conceals *for us!*

76

"The glory of kings is to
search out a matter."
—Proverbs 25:2

We are kings and priests to our God (see Rev. 1:6).

Our royal identity never shines brighter than when we pursue hidden things with the confidence that we have legal access to such things.

Mysteries are our inheritance.

Our kingship, our role in ruling and reigning with Christ, comes to the forefront when we seek Him for answers to the dilemmas of the world around us.

77

"To you it has been granted to know the mysteries of the kingdom of heaven, but to them it has not been granted."
—Matthew 13:11 NASB

We, as believers, have legal access to the realm of God's mysteries. It's that simple.

The hidden things are placed in waiting for the believer to discover.

They are ours by inheritance.

78

A KINGDOM PERSPECTIVE

It is very hard to imagine the Church bringing answers to the issues of life when much of our eschatology anticipates world conditions getting worse and worse.

When we also believe that the darkness of world circumstances is the signal for Christ's return, we have a conflict that ultimately costs us a practical vision—to invade and transform the world system.

79

Jesus is returning for a spotless Bride, whose Body is in equal proportion to her Head.

The Father alone knows when that moment will be. We don't. Our job is to do everything possible to bring about, *"Thy kingdom come, Thy will be done, on earth as it is in Heaven."*

80

ANSWERS FOR THE HOUR

If my faith for His return has its anchor in the darkness of the world around me, then I will do little to change it. We will try to get converts, of course, but to bring answers to the issues of this planet will not be a priority. Yet this is the practical tool that turns the hearts of the kings of our day.

"Do you see a man who excels in his work?
He will stand before kings;
He will not stand before unknown men."
—PROVERBS 22:29

81

Commissioned to Disciple Nations

Our commission is clear: We are to disciple nations! And to insure that this seemingly impossible task would be possible, He caused the One called "The Desire of the Nations" to live within us.

This revelation of Him is ultimately a revelation about us, for we are His Body. Being made in His image gives us the privilege and responsibility to reflect His greatness to the world around us. The nations are looking for a people who can bring the answers to the issues facing our world.

82

THE PURPOSE OF A PROMISE

Hannah's womb was closed. She was barren and without hope of bearing children apart from a miracle. As cruel as it may sound to the natural man, God used this to bring her into her greatest success. In her barrenness she developed a desperate heart.

To embrace the privilege of creative expression is consistent with being made in the image and likeness of our Creator.

This means that barrenness in any area is our invitation to excel.

83

"An inheritance gained hurriedly at the beginning will not be blessed in the end."
—Proverbs 20:21 NASB

Not everything comes to us easily, nor should it. The God who hides things for us also gives us His Kingdom as our inheritance.

Israel was given the Promised Land but was told it would come to them little by little so that the beasts wouldn't become too numerous for them. His promises cover everything—His promises are *yes and amen!* (See 2 Corinthians 1:20.) All is covered by the redemptive work on the Cross, but it is gained little by little, sometimes through our co-laboring effort.

THE EVER-EXPANDING KINGDOM

It is true that a full manifestation of the Kingdom of God is more than our physical bodies can endure. But it is also true that when we are in Heaven we will still be able to say *now, but not yet* about the Kingdom, because there is no end to the increase of His government.

Throughout eternity the Kingdom will be expanding, and we will always be advancing.

85

The Tense of the Kingdom

If the concept of Kingdom-now, but-not-yet is used to define promise and potential, accept it.

If it is spoken to build awareness of our limitations and restrictions, reject it.

We don't need more people without authentic Kingdom experiences telling us what we can and cannot have in our lifetime. Those who walk out their faith with an experiential paradigm understand that we will always live in the tension of what we have seen and what we have yet to see, and that we are always moving on to *more* in God. This is an *understanding by experience* issue.

Part Four

THE LANGUAGE OF THE SPIRIT

It is vital to learn how God speaks. His first language is not English. In fact, it would be safe to say it's not Hebrew either. While He uses the languages of men to communicate with us, He is more inclined to speak through a myriad of other methods.

86

A yielded imagination becomes a sanctified imagination; and it's the sanctified imagination that is positioned for visions and dreams.

The imagination is like a canvas to a painter. If it's clean, the artist has much to work with.

God would love to use our imagination to paint His impressions upon; He just looks for those who are yielded.

However, those who are preoccupied with "not being worthy" are too self-centered to be trusted with much revelation. At some point it has to stop being about us long enough to utilize the benefits of being in Christ for the sake of those around us. Such a position gives us unlimited access to the mysteries of God that enable us to touch the needs of a dying world.

Jesus is the Word of God. It's hard for Him to not have something to say.

Occasionally, we go through times when we feel God is not speaking to us. While that may be so, most of the time He has simply changed His language, and He expects us to adjust with Him.

89

Wisdom's Counterfeit

One of my greatest concerns for the Church in the Western world is the prevalence of unbelief.

It has masqueraded long enough as wisdom and must be exposed for being the great sin that it is.

Unbelief has the outward appearance of a conservative approach to life, but works to subject God Himself to the mind and control of people. It feeds off the opinion of others, all the while stroking itself for not falling into the extremes that others have stumbled into. What is seldom realized by those who live in such a religious trap is that an unbelieving mindset is completely unable to represent Jesus in His power and glory.

90

FREEDOM FROM UNREASONABLE CAUTION

It is grievous to see an empty wheelchair with someone walking, a formerly depressed person rejoicing, or one who could not hear now hearing and giving praise while the bystander still wants proof those were really miracles. I realize that charlatans exist. But the massive effort to protect ourselves from being fooled is more a sign of unbelief than it is of our wisdom keeping us from deception. Such a fear only exists where unbelief has reigned for a long time.

However, *"Love believes all things"* (1 Cor. 13:7 NASB).

A deeper encounter with the love of God frees a person from the tendency to protect themselves out of fear through unreasonable caution.

91

HIS VOICE IS LIFE

I am strengthened in hearing God speak. I am nourished through my own obedience to His voice. The situations of life take on meaning and purpose because of the abiding faith to follow Jesus.

Hearing from God is the essential element of the Christian life, for *"man shall not live by bread alone, but by every word that proceeds from the mouth of God"* (Matt. 4:4).

His voice is our life.

THE TABLE OF GOD'S WILL

There are many tables to eat at in life. There is the table of *public opinion.* The food is sweet, but it sours in the stomach. There is the table of *personal achievement.* That's a power meal for sure, yet the crash is as rapid as the ascent.

There's only one table with rich food that settles well and brings supernatural strength—it's the table of God's will.

"My food is to do the will of Him who sent me."
—JOHN 4:34 NASB

93

LEARNING THE SPIRIT'S LANGUAGE

The beauty of God's will is lost for the person who does not know the language of the Spirit.

It is vital to learn how God speaks. His first language is not English. In fact, it would be safe to say it's not Hebrew either. While He uses the languages of men to communicate with us, He is more inclined to speak through a myriad of other methods.

94

The Scriptures are the basis for all "hearing" from God.

While God will not violate His Word, He often violates our understanding of His Word.

Remember, God is bigger than His book. The Bible does not contain God; it *reveals Him.*

95

THE BIBLE AND HIS VOICE

Bible reading is the most common way of receiving instruction and learning to recognize His voice. Page after page is filled with practical instructions for life. Learning the principles of God's Word helps us to learn to recognize His voice by establishing truth in our hearts.

The Psalmist affirmed that purpose, saying, *"Your word I have treasured in my heart, that I may not sin against You"* (Ps. 119:11 NASB). This is where we find the Kingdom principles for life. They work for anyone who applies them.

96

THE SPOKEN WORD

Rhema is the freshly spoken word. It is always an expression of that which is being uttered. Therefore it carries an aspect of immediacy with it. Oftentimes God breathes upon His Word and gives life to something written for "now." The spoken word is never to replace the written Word.

The more of the written Word we have in our hearts, the greater capacity we have to hear the spoken word, because He speaks to that which has been deposited in our hearts and calls it forth.

97

The Audible Voice

The voice of the Lord is not an impression that we have to find language for. It is a direct word-for-word communication from God to us. The audible voice may come to the natural ear while we're awake or while we're asleep. It can also come to our spiritual ears.

98

STILL SMALL VOICE

This is the quiet voice or impression of the heart. This is probably the most common way that people hear from God. It is sometimes thought to be our own "inner voice" in that it is our own thoughts and ideas. While we do have such a voice, it is wisdom to learn to recognize *His* still small voice. It is quiet. So we must become quiet to recognize it consistently. Someone gave me a helpful clue to discerning His voice; they said, "You know you've heard from God whenever you have an idea that's better than one you could think up yourself."

99

Language of Dark Sayings

God sometimes speaks to us by hiding truths in phrases, stories, riddles, and circumstances. The meaning is there for us to find. When we *lean into God,* anticipating His voice, it becomes easier to discern when those circumstances are from God or are merely unusual events in life. This unique language from God is an invitation to enter His great adventure.

100

PAY ATTENTION TO THE UNUSUAL

There are highly unusual situations that usually seem to have no meaning in and of themselves. God brings those events into our lives to get our attention, hoping we will "turn aside" from our agendas and plans.

"When the Lord saw that he turned aside
to look, God called to him from the midst
of the bush and said, 'Moses, Moses!'"
—EXODUS 3:4 NASB

To embrace the privilege of creative expression is consistent with being made in the image and likeness of our Creator.

101

THE LANGUAGE OF PROPHECY

To encourage risk on the part of prophetic people, we emphasize the responsibility of the hearer to discern whether or not a word is from God. In the Old Testament the Spirit of God was upon the prophet alone, so he bore all the responsibility.

Today the Spirit of the Lord is within every believer, so the responsibility is now given to the people of God to discern whether or not a specific word is from God. When it is from God, we respond according to the direction given in the Word. When it's not from God, we try to learn from it and sharpen our prophetic skills.

102

OUR RESPONSE TO PROPHECY

Prophecy comes to us from another person. While this can be a very dangerous form of hearing from God, it can also be one of the most dramatic and faith building. Once it has been confirmed as having its origins from God, we must act accordingly.

103

TESTIMONY

"The testimony of Jesus is the spirit of prophecy."
—REVELATION 19:10 NASB

The spoken or written record of whatever Jesus has done carries the prophetic anointing to cause a change in events in the spirit realm so that the miracle spoken of can happen again.

Indeed, a testimony often carries the actual voice of the Lord. Learning to recognize it will enable us to accommodate and cooperate with the move of His Spirit that was released in the testimony.

Part Five

Invading Babylon

Any gospel that doesn't work in the marketplace doesn't work.

104

DEFINING KINGDOM AUTHORITY

We have been given authority over this planet. It was first given to us in the commission God gave to mankind in Genesis (see Gen. 1:28-29) and was then restored to us by Jesus after His resurrection (see Matt. 28:18).

But Kingdom authority is different than is typically understood by many believers. It is the authority to set people free from torment and disease, destroying the works of darkness. It is the authority to move the resources of Heaven through creative expression to meet human need. It is the authority to bring Heaven to earth. It is the authority to serve.

105

Stewarding Authority Through Service

The truths of humanity's dominion and authority are dangerous in the hands of those who desire to rule over others. These concepts seem to validate some people's selfishness.

But when these truths are expressed through the humble servant, the world is rocked to its core.

Becoming servants to this world is the key to open the doors of possibility that are generally thought of as closed or forbidden.

106

Servant and King

Neither our understanding of servants or of kings can help us much with this challenge, for both are soiled in our world, probably beyond repair.

That is where Jesus comes in. He is the King of all kings, yet the Servant of all. This unique combination found in the Son of God is the call of the hour upon us.

107

"The earth cannot bear up under a slave when he becomes king."
—see PROVERBS 30:21-22

As truth is usually found in the tension of two conflicting realities, we have an issue to solve. Like our Master we are both royalty and servants (see Rev. 1:5; Mark 10:45). Solomon warns us of this problem in Proverbs 30.

Yet Jesus contradicted Solomon's warning, without nullifying the statement, by being effective at both.

108

Jesus served with the heart of a king, but ruled with the heart of a servant.

This is the essential combination that must be embraced by those longing to shape the course of history.

109

Royalty is my identity. Servanthood is my assignment. Intimacy with God is my life source. So, before God, I'm an intimate. Before people, I'm a servant. Before the powers of hell, I'm a ruler, with no tolerance for their influence.

Wisdom knows which role to fulfill at the proper time.

110

The dominion of the Lord Jesus is manifest whenever the people of God go forth to serve by bringing the order and blessing of His world into this one.

111

SERVANT LEADERS

The effort by many believers to simply obtain positions of leadership is putting the cart before the horse. Servanthood remains our strong suit, and it's through service that we can bring the benefits of His world into the reach of the common man.

112

LEAVEN OF THE KINGDOM

The Kingdom is likened unto leaven (see Matt. 13:33). As yeast has an effect on the dough it is "worked into," so we will transform all the kingdoms of this world as we are worked into its systems. From there we must display His dominion and rule.

As the people of God move into these realms of society to show forth the benefits and values of the Kingdom, His government expands.

113

There is no such thing as secular employment for the believer. Once we are born again, everything about us is redeemed for Kingdom purposes.

It is all spiritual.

It is either a legitimate Kingdom expression, or we shouldn't be involved at all.

114

Every believer is in full-time ministry—only a few have pulpits in sanctuaries. The rest have their pulpit in their areas of expertise and favor in the world system.

Be sure to preach only good news. And when necessary, use words!

115

The call of God is important, not because of the title it carries (or doesn't carry). It's valuable because of the One who called us.

116

EMBRACE YOUR KINGDOM ASSIGNMENT

An assignment to be in business is as valuable in the Kingdom as is the call to be an evangelist. The privilege to be a stay-at-home wife and mother is equal in importance to being a missionary.

Embrace your call with the faithfulness and thankfulness worthy of the One who has called you.

117

Eternal Rewards

Our eternal rewards do not come because of how much money we made, how many souls were saved, or how many homeless people we fed.

All rewards are given based on our faithfulness to what God has given and called us to be and to do.

HONORING FAITHFULNESS

The honor we give to one another must not be only to those who have obvious spiritual occupations.

Honor must be given to those who are faithful in the call, no matter what it is.

FIND THE GOLD

Prophetic ministry is not to be focused on the sins of the world. It takes very little discernment to find the dirt in people's lives.

> **The prophetic in its purest form is designed to find the gold in people's lives and call it to the surface.**

120

COVERT MINISTRY

The word *covert* means "hiding place." This refers to ministry that is more subtle in nature. It is hidden not because of cowardice but rather out of wisdom.

It works within the systems of this world to bring about change by reestablishing the proper norms of thought, beliefs, disciplines, and relational boundaries.

121

Serving with No Strings Attached

The Church is sometimes known for its willingness to serve, but usually with well-meaning spiritual agendas as the ultimate goal. It almost sounds blasphemous, but serving simply to get people saved is a religious agenda. As pure and noble as it may seem to us as believers, it is manipulative to the world and is viewed as impure service. The world can smell it a mile away. We put them on the defensive when we carry such reasons for serving into their sphere of responsibility.

But, for example, when we volunteer in our local school to help the principal succeed, then we've crossed the line into territory seldom visited by the Church. It is serving for the benefit of another. It's that kind of a servant whom the world welcomes. The amazing bonus is you also end up influencing the school in ways you never thought possible, including bringing people to Christ.

122

What would happen if we actually invaded the systems of this world to give honor where it is due instead of dishonoring those whom we think deserve expulsion?

123

A Generation Called to Transform Society

It is obvious that God wants an entire generation to value their call regardless of what title it brings, teaching them how to invade a culture for its total and complete transformation. God fully intends for there to be a fulfillment of His Word about *"the kingdoms of this world have become the kingdoms of our Lord"* (Rev. 11:15).

124

DISPLAYING THE MIND OF GOD

It is the display of the mind of God always in the context of integrity that brings forth the creative solutions for life while holding to the standards of excellence. These play a vital role in manifesting the Kingdom in ways that honor God and solve the issues of life for humankind.

Business

125

KINGDOM SUCCESS

People instinctively want both—outward and inward success. The Kingdom businessperson has the chance to display a more complete picture of success by focusing not only on money. Their celebration of life, with all its many facets, will grab the attention of those hopelessly trapped in the "money is success" daily grind.

126

The Testimony of Divine Order

While there is room for overt ministry in every part of life, it is generally not the outward preaching of the Gospel that secures the place of favor in the eyes of the unbelieving businessperson.

It is divine order (Kingdom) in the overall approach to life—to self, family, business, and community.

127

UNLOCKING KINGDOM CREATIVITY

Creativity is a necessary component for the Kingdom businessperson. It brings fresh ideas that keep adventure as a central part of their assignment. Witty inventions are going to increase in the Christian community, as God is using that expression of wisdom to bring about a transfer of wealth for Kingdom purposes.

128

Do you see a man who excels in his work? He will stand before kings; He will not stand before unknown men.
—Proverbs 22:29

This verse tells us two things: One, the result of lives pursuing excellence—they will influence the influencers.

Two, kings demand excellence. Many compromise in this area to make a quick buck, but it is excellence that provides wealth for the long term. It's a wealth that has no sorrow (see Prov. 10:22).

Excellence is a Kingdom value and is not to be confused with perfectionism, which is a counterfeit and comes from the religious spirit. One of the clearest paths of promotion is through excellence.

EDUCATION

129

Oftentimes the Church reacts to the abuses of the world system and creates an error equal in danger to one we've rejected.

130

Exchange Rejection for Transformation

The Western mindset, which values reason as the only proper measure of truth, has undermined the Gospel. This worldview, which Paul battled in First Corinthians, has been embraced by our educational culture. It is anti-Christ in nature. The supernatural then becomes subject to the evaluation of ignorant people. But the solution to this problem is not to reject education; the answer is to invade. Our rejection removes us from our place of preservation as "*the salt of the earth*" (Matt. 5:13).

131

God is willing to debate anyone. He is very secure in His understanding and arguments. He also backs up His insights with evidence that will bear up under scrutiny.

132

A System That Shapes Minds

Invading the educational system is essential as it's this mountain that greatly shapes the minds and expectations of the younger generation. While it could be argued that today entertainers have a greater role in shaping the minds of the young, it is the educators who generally shape the minds of the entertainers in their way of thinking.

133

Restoring Esteem for Positions in Society

Too many generations who experience the outpouring of the Spirit forfeit their desires for training and education in order to do "the Lord's work." As noble as that sounds, it comes from a misunderstanding of real ministry aided by the idea that we will be taken out of here at any moment.

This is a tender subject, as we must be ready to be with the Lord at any given moment. But as the Church regains the value for *no job is secular for the believer,* the esteem will return for the positions in society that had little value in prior generations.

134

The desire for Heaven is right and healthy.

But it must not replace our commission: *"Your kingdom come. Your will be done, on earth as it is in heaven"* (Matt. 6:10 NASB).

135

OCCUPY UNTIL HE COMES

We were not commissioned to look into the clouds for His coming (see Acts 1:11). We were commanded to "occupy" until He comes (Luke 19:13 KJV). *Occupy* is a military term. And according to Kingdom values, occupation is *always* for the purpose of advancement.

136

Educating the Next Generation

Our children must become educated and become educators. But that goal is not complete without the Kingdom mindset. We are sending them into dangerous territory to get their training. Choose their schools carefully. Each teacher who trains your child is a delegated authority—delegated by you.

The Bible does not give the authority for training children to the government, no matter how noble their intent. It rests upon your shoulders, so pray, pray, pray, and educate, educate, educate.

137

Training Our Children

We would never send our child to a restaurant where only one in ten die of food poisoning. Yet we do that daily in our educational system, with odds that are much worse than one in ten. We often send them out, unguarded, into a system that works to undermine faith and ultimately their relationship with God.

The answer is not to withdraw from society and move into the mountains to preserve the family unit. The answer is to train and invade. Our training is superior to theirs if it's authentic, because it is driven by a personal relationship with God and includes transforming divine encounters.

HEAVEN'S SOLUTIONS FOR DAILY NEEDS

Most people in our culture unknowingly live under the influence of a dark kingdom. Yet they suffer with problems that have their answer in the Kingdom of God and the believer. Both wisdom and power are available to us that we might provide solutions from another world that meet their needs.

139

When God's people step forward to serve, God backs it up with power.

140

ACCESS TO UNSEEN REALMS

Moral values are the basis for integrity.

And moral values are rooted in the character of God.

The supernatural educator has access to a realm of stability that others don't have.

That is not to say one has to be a believer to have integrity. Many unbelievers do. But the supernatural element available in the realm of character is reserved for those who have the Spirit of the resurrected Christ living in them.

141

Words That Produce Fruit

Young people need educators with integrity, but they also need those who believe in them. Calling out the treasure in a young person can mark them for good forever. Oftentimes such an educator plants a seed that another person will harvest, but that is the joy of this Kingdom—no words return void.

"It is the same with my word.
I send it out, and it always produces fruit.
It will accomplish all I want it to,
and it will prosper everywhere I send it."
—Isaiah 55:11 NLT

142

SECRET AND SUPERIOR ANSWERS

There are answers to every problem we face.

There are methods of training people that are far superior to what we know now.

Kingdom-oriented people, who know who they are in Christ, will access these secrets for the benefit of all who are around them.

143

Excellence is more than exhorting students to get good grades. It is a gift from God that uses the full measure of resources from both the natural and spiritual realities.

144

SUMMONING THE EXCELLENCE WITHIN

Each person has an area where God has gifted them to excel, and it's the wise educator who discovers that area in a child. An excellent teacher will bring excellence out of the one who can't find it in themselves.

Entertainment

145

The Church has often fallen to the notion that darkness is stronger than light.

146

Light Invading Darkness

Entertainment is a mountain of influence that must be invaded. The indictment of that realm being "unholy" was accurate, but unfortunately it is also a self-fulfilling prophecy.

Anywhere we do not invade becomes darker in our absence.

We are the "*light of the world*" (Matt. 5:14).

147

The realms of society that we fail to invade are hopelessly lost to darkness. Invasion is the responsibility of light.

148

HEAVENLY ACCESS...NOW

Heaven has what we want.

Every creative dream is fulfilled in Heaven.

The great news is that we have access to that realm through prayers of faith.

149

SOUNDS IN HEAVEN

There are sounds in Heaven that earth has never heard.

When a musician taps into that reality and communicates that sound here, Heaven will have found agreement and will invade.

150

Art Originates in God

All art finds its origins in the person of God; more specifically, it's found in His holiness. The Scripture says, *"in the beauty of holiness"* (Ps. 29:2).

It's tragic that holiness gets such poor treatment from the people of God. It is God's nature, His person. Beauty pours forth from that one attribute.

"And when he had consulted with the people,
he appointed those who should sing to the Lord,
and who should praise the beauty of holiness."
—2 Chronicles 20:21

151

THE BEACON OF INTEGRITY

In crisis, people will always turn to those who are stable.

Integrity will be a beacon of light to those wandering through this land of disappointment and shame.

152

Anyone who has escaped the pressure to duplicate trash will automatically be positioned to create.

153

SUPERNATURAL CREATIVE ADVANTAGE

Learning how to pray in the Spirit and *soak* in His presence will give great advantages to those wanting to invade the entertainment mountain.

Heaven has what we're looking for.

And you'll have to go there to get it.

154

The best novels and plays have yet to be written. The most beautiful melodies to ever grace the human ear are yet to be discovered.

Those with an ear for God, discovering the experience of "being seated in heavenly places," will have access to things no other generation has ever seen before.

155

COUNTERFEIT CREATIVITY

Many have mistakenly thought that the devil has all the good music.

He is not creative.

Tragically, he receives credit for too many things, even by the Church.

156

CREATIVE BY DIVINE DESIGN

How is it that an ungodly person can write a beautiful piece of music or a brilliant script for a movie?

How is it they can paint a masterpiece or design buildings that take our breath away?

They were made in the image of God, and He doesn't remove that distinguishing feature when a person rebels against Him.

CHURCH

157

SOMETHING COMES ALIVE!

Many in the religious community have a lot of sincerity.

When they see someone who actually practices the purity and power from the pages of Scripture, something comes alive in them.

They hope it's true.

They just lack examples.

158

Being committed to another leader's success, with no personal agenda for gain, is essential for invasion into the church mountain.

159

True Kingdom Success

Ignoring the external measurements of success will enable the leader in this realm to value what the King values—passion, purity, power, and people.

160

RIGHTEOUS PEER PRESSURE

Righteous people can provide a righteous peer pressure.

When fellowship becomes valuable enough that it is sacrificial, then those in fellowship begin to walk in the light—openly, with integrity and accountability.

161

While change for change's sake is not always healthy, those resistant to change are usually resistant to the Holy Spirit.

162

If anyone should be known for creativity, it should be those in whom the accurate image of the Creator has been formed—born-again believers.

Cultural relevance is rightfully the cry of the hour, but it must be relevance with power!

164

THE HIGH ROAD OF EXCELLENCE

The Church has often taken the low road in the realm of excellence because of a misunderstanding of humility.

But the choice of that road usually flows from low faith, and humility gets the blame.

Excellence can and must be the expression of true humility as humility declares, "Our best, for His glory!"

165

Most of the areas that can bring the greatest results have the greatest risk. This is no exception.

Excellence is Kingdom.

Perfectionism is religion.

Poverty is demonic.

FAMILY

166

Healthy and Not Hidden

All a family needs to do to have influence in this mountain is to be healthy and not hidden.

167

Influence Without Limits

When relationships are good and the boundaries of godly disciplines are intact, there is no limit to the influence of the Christian home.

168

SALT AND LIGHT

The problem has often been a false standard of holiness wherein the Christian doesn't associate with the unbeliever, yet maintains similar values and habits to them.

The opposite should be our goal—mingle and associate with the lost, but don't take on their values or habits.

That way we, as both salt and light, have our proper effect of preserving and exposing in order to bring them into their destiny.

Healthy families that are intentional breed healthy families.

170

Reproducing Godly Character

When parents have godly character and wisdom for raising children, they produce a family that reflects the love and integrity of Christ.

171

BEHIND CLOSED DOORS

If children grow up seeing one standard in church and another at home, they tend to rebel against standards all together. Conversely, when integrity is genuine both in and out of the public eye, children grow up willing to pay the price needed to follow in their parents' footsteps, as long as they have been given room for individuality.

172

EMBRACE THE ADVENTURE

Few families actually purposely live the adventure of life together.

Embracing such an adventure together is what gives place for creative expression to surface.

173

MEASURING EXCELLENCE

Excellence can't be measured in buying the finest car or the most expensive clothes.

Rather it is displayed in our approach to life—all of us, for all of Him.

Government

174

There is a new breed being groomed for this hour who fears only God and lives with a wisdom that enables one to dance through the minefield of public opinion.

175

A PROVERB A DAY

Reading a chapter a day in the Book of Proverbs, according to the date, will give leaders in the realm of government a compass bearing so that no issue arises that doesn't have a Kingdom solution.

176

FOR THE BENEFIT OF THE WHOLE

The Word of God remains true—"*when it goes well with the righteous, the city rejoices*" (Prov. 11:10). People instinctively want to be governed by people who are honest and righteous.

They want leaders who are not self-serving but will actually govern sacrificially for the benefit of the whole.

177

We need to embrace the standard of Jesus—serve like a king and rule like a servant.

178

BASIC ROLES OF GOVERNMENT

Two of the most basic roles of government are to create a realm of safety and a realm of prosperity.

When governmental leaders use their position for personal gain, it amounts to prostituting their charisma for themselves.

Excellence is found in doing our best for the sake of others.

Science and Medicine

We are praying that the righteous are assigned to those places of influence, because we want to make it nearly impossible to get to hell from our city.

180

Facing Eternity, Receptive to Truth

You've heard the saying, *there are no atheists in foxholes*—the same could be said of those on the edge of eternity.

People are very receptive to the Truth when they are facing death.

181

AUTHENTIC LOVE AND COMPASSION

Authentic love and compassion for people, expressed by those planted within that system, brings forth a wonderful harvest.

It's amazing what we are allowed to do when we *go in low just to serve.*

182

People know the difference between authentic love and a person fulfilling their religious obligations. Real love has very few opponents.

183

Christlike character always puts others first.

184

Medicine and Healing

It's a beautiful combination when we see a whole segment of society raised up that can work in both the natural and the supernatural realms to bring about good health.

185

**As wonderful as healing is,
divine health is greater.**

Access to Superior Promises

Believers have been given access to the mysteries of the Kingdom regarding this subject.

It would be tragic to come to the end of time and have the only generation to experience divine health be the Israelites. They lived under an inferior covenant and were in rebellion against God.

Inferior covenants cannot make superior promises.

187

Those in the mountain of science and medicine have access to things that the entire world is aggressively asking for.

Asking God for specific solutions will enable those involved in medicine to give true creative expression to a dying world.

188

Passion wears out when it relies solely on self-motivation.

**God has fire in His eyes!
Frequent encounters with Him
will keep any flame in us burning.**

Part Six

The Practical Side of Things

If it matters to you, it matters to Him.

190

NO ONE BESIDES HIM

Perhaps you've heard it said, *God is number one, the family is number two, and the Church is number three.* That unofficial list is important as it outlines a few of the priorities in a Christian's life that have become confused through the years. I know of many tragedies in pastors' families because they ignored these priorities of Kingdom living. Yet, as good as this list is, I don't believe it is technically accurate.

When God is number one, there is no number two.

191

His Love Flows Through Us

Out of my love for God I give myself to my wife and kids.

It's not separate from the Lord, but it is unto Him.

It's not that I can't love my wife without loving God—many unbelievers do that well.

But in knowing and loving God, I am released to a measure of supernatural love that is unattainable apart from God.

192

It should be said that anyone who is completely abandoned to God should love others more than they thought possible.

193

Expressions of Love

My love for God *is* my love for life. They cannot be separated.

Loving my family, church, ministry…is an expression of my love for God.

God being number one, the only One.

194

Religion is destructive because it implies that only overtly spiritual activities are acceptable as service to God and that anything that doesn't have to do with Bible reading, witnessing, church attendance, etc. is not true Christian service.

195

No Room for a Dual Life

Religion takes us back to the concept of spiritual and secular parts of the Christian life. The person living this dual life needs a list of priorities to survive; otherwise they will not take care of other matters of importance.

Their concept of God doesn't allow them to actually have a passion for something that is not viewed as a Christian discipline.

196

PASSION FOR GOD BIRTHS PASSION

We must have a shift in thinking whereby we recognize that passion for God *gives birth to a passion for other things.*

And it's those other things that are often to be pursued as unto the Lord.

197

A Picture of Love

Scripture reminds us that if we love God it will be measurable by our love for people.

This is such an absolute principle that God says if we don't love others, we don't actually love Him.

The point is this: In the wake of our passion for God, passion for other things is created.

It is often in giving ourselves to those things that we prove and manifest our love for God.

"If anyone boasts, 'I love God,' and goes right on hating his brother or sister, thinking nothing of it, he is a liar. If he won't love the person he can see, how can he love the God he can't see? The command we have from Christ is blunt: Loving God includes loving people. You've got to love both."
—1 John 4:20-21 MSG

198

While some worship nature, I worship the One it points to—the Creator.

"But the basic reality of God is plain enough. Open your eyes and there it is! By taking a long and thoughtful look at what God has created, people have always been able to see what their eyes as such can't see: eternal power, for instance, and the mystery of his divine being."
—Romans 1:20 MSG

199

My love for my family, for hunting and fishing, the mountains and the ocean, fountain pens, and French roast coffee are all part of the enjoyment of life for me; and that joy is born completely through a relationship with Him.

"The heavens are telling of the glory of God; and their expanse is declaring the work of His hands. Day to day pours forth speech, and night to night reveals knowledge."
—Psalms 19:1-2 NASB

200

While it is possible to value other things above God, it is not possible to value God without valuing other things.

201

A Good Steward of Life

The effort to accomplish the goal of loving God with no other passions has had to create a monastic lifestyle to survive. And while I admire many of the monastic believers in the past, it is not the model that Jesus gave us.

The way we steward the rest of life becomes the litmus test that demonstrates an authentic love for God.

202

THE PRAYER LIST

Like most people, I have a list of things I pray for.

They represent the basic desires and needs of my life and those I love.

If they're not written down on paper, they're at least written in my heart.

On the list are things which have obvious eternal significance—prayer for our cities, for the salvation of certain people we've ministered to, for healing breakthrough in tough cases, provision—both personal and the church.

Following the urgent is the "it would be nice" section of the list. It is long and has varying degrees of importance. But I've noticed that God sometimes bypasses the list and goes directly to the "I haven't even bothered to ask" part that dwells somewhere deep in my heart.

It is a pleasant and sometimes offensive move.

203

My prayer requests are important, but my view of Him is more important.

204

REVEALING THE FATHER

God bypassing my "urgent" prayer list, my "it would be nice" list, and entering the "secret desires of the heart" list told me more about my heavenly Father than answering all the other things I had been praying about.

205

Unlimited Power

People frequently come asking me to pray with them for someone else's healing.

Sometimes they have an obvious physical need themselves, but will ask for their friend's healing instead. When I press them about their own condition, they usually say something like, "Oh, I'd rather have God heal them than me. They have cancer. I only have a ruptured disc in my back." Their compassion is wonderful because they are putting another person's need before their own. But their concept of God is wrong. Really wrong!

He doesn't have limited power.

In other words, He won't run out of power after He heals their back.

He'll still have enough power left to heal their friend's cancer.

206

UNDIVIDED ATTENTION

With God, you don't just get one wish and run out after the first one is used up.

The desire for someone else's breakthrough is noble, but it's not an "either/or" situation.

Besides that, God's attention span is excellent; so good in fact that He can give His undivided attention to every human being on the planet, all at the same time.

207

God's Logic

God does not view our prayers on the same priority scale that we do.

Some would see it this way: "Of course God heals cancer. That's important. My ruptured disc is not as important. I have learned to live with it."

We think of cancer being urgent (which it is) and everything else should be put on hold.

In reality, it's often the blown disc that gets healed first. And the increase of faith in that one experience helps to bring about the faith needed for healing of the cancer.

Our logic is not consistent with His, and He isn't going to change.

208

Creative Kingdom influence can and must be demonstrated in all we do, big and small.

209

How and what we communicate has the potential to change the atmosphere, creating the context for people to be released to their destiny.

ANOINTED WORDS

Our communication skills must come under the influence of the Holy Spirit.

Done correctly, our words are able to release the presence of God into people's lives through the expressions of compassion and concern.

211

SOLUTIONS FROM HEAVEN

To consistently bring Kingdom solutions to the forefront of society, we will have to learn how to access the realm of Heaven; for it is in Heaven where our answers lie.

Part Seven

THE SPIRIT OF REVELATION

We thrive with the spirit of revelation, but we perish without it.

212

SEEING THE UNSEEN

People who see what is unseen have the advantage over everyone else who desires a place of significance.

They are the ones who are able to *live from Heaven toward earth.*

213

When we live conscious of Heaven and eternity, it changes the way we live and radically increases our measure of impact on society.

214

The ones who see Heaven most clearly have little desire for this world, yet they are the ones who have the greatest impact on the world around them.

215

"Set your mind on the things above,
not on the things that are on earth.
For you have died and your life is
hidden with Christ in God."
—Colossians 3:2-3 NASB

The abundant life that Jesus promised to His disciples is found in this unseen realm.

216

BRINGING HEAVEN TO EARTH

The display of Jesus's dominion through miracles and various supernatural expressions are all rooted in the heavenly world. We must access His world to change this one.

217

Signs Leading Us into New Territory

Changing the course of world history is our assignment. Yet we have gone as far as we can with what we presently know. We need signs to get where we want to go.

Signs are realities that point to a greater reality. An exit sign is real, but it points to something greater—the exit.

218

SIGNS THAT RESTORE WONDER

We don't need signs when we travel on familiar roads.

But if we're going to go where we've never gone before, we'll need signs to get there.

These *signs* will restore the *wonder.*

219

The Great Need of the Hour

To go any further we need to hear from God anew.

We must see the things that are before our faces day after day, yet are presently hidden from our eyes.

The ever-present need to see and hear has never been greater.

The key to staying current with the shifting seasons of God is the spirit of revelation.

220

PRAYING FOR THE ONE WHO HAS "EVERYTHING"

What do you give to the one who has everything?

> **Prayer for their eyes to open to see what is still unseen (revelation), and the insight to know what to do with it once they see it (wisdom).**

221

THERE'S ALWAYS MORE

Even a church in revival, known for great teaching and citywide impact, needs more revelation.

It is not automatic.

222

TALKING ABOUT IT IS NOT ENOUGH

To say, "The Spirit of God is welcome here, and free to do as He pleases" is not enough.

Many of the things we need and long for must be prayed for specifically and pursued relentlessly.

Such is the case with the spirit of wisdom and revelation.

223

Only when wisdom and revelation are passionately pursued do they take the place they deserve in the Christian life.

224

These two elements—wisdom and revelation—become the safeguards that keep us from the peril of religion.

225

DISCERNING THE DIFFERENCE

What I know will help me.

What I think I know will hurt me.

It's the spirit of revelation that helps me know the difference.

226

REVELATION FOR CRUCIAL MOMENTS

The prophets warned us about what would happen to a people who did not increase in knowledge through revelation.

All knowledge is useful, but it can be general. But when God releases revelation, it releases knowledge that enables us to address specific issues at crucial moments.

227

It can be said that we thrive with revelation knowledge... but perish without it.

228

BUSY...BUT SEPARATED

Without revelation we are completely cut off from the purposes of God on the earth.

It is possible to be busy about the Lord's work, yet still separated from His purposes.

229

ACCESSING HEAVEN'S SIGHT

We are unfit to carry the weightiness of such a responsibility—fulfilling God's purposes—apart from the spirit of revelation working in our lives.

It is costly to have access to *sight* and not use it.

230

THE KNOWLEDGE OF INTIMACY

"My people are destroyed for lack of knowledge."
—HOSEA 4:6 NASB

Knowledge in this context is experiential knowledge. It is more than mere concepts or theories. The word knowledge here comes from the word used in Genesis describing the experience of intimacy: *"And Adam knew Eve his wife; and she conceived and bare Cain"* (Gen. 4:1 KJV).

231

While the Bible is complete (no more books are to be added) it is a closed book without the help of the Holy Spirit.

We must have revelation to see what is already written.

232

EXPERIENCING TRUTH

We know so little of what God wants us to understand from His Word.

Jesus said as much.

He couldn't teach His disciples all that was in His heart (see John 16:12).

This is the knowledge that comes from the Spirit of God as He breathes upon the pages of Scripture. It leads to divine encounters; truth experienced is never forgotten.

233

Where there is no revelation,
the people cast off restraint.
—Proverbs 29:18

Many have thought this passage was about goals and dreams. It's not!

It's about the impact of the spirit of revelation upon a person's life, enabling them to joyfully restrain themselves from everything that works against the dream of God for us.

234

MULTIDIMENSIONAL TRUTH

Not all truth is equal. Truth is multidimensional—some things are true, and some things are truer.

If you touched a leper in the Old Testament, you became unclean. A primary revelation of the Old Testament is the power of sin. In the New Testament you touch the leper and the leper becomes clean. A primary revelation of the New Testament is the power of God's love.

Both statements are true (*sin is powerful* and *love is powerful)* but one is clearly superior.

235

Revelation for the Season

The Holy Spirit has been given to lead us into all truth. But one of the things He is so clearly in charge of is taking us into the truths that the Father wants emphasized in a particular season.

236

"For this reason I will not be negligent to remind you always of these things, though you know and are established in the present truth."
—2 PETER 1:12

Present truth implies truth that is at the forefront of God's thinking.

It is a wise man who learns to recognize where the winds of Heaven are blowing. Life and ministry are so much easier when we involve ourselves in what God is already blessing.

238

LIVING IN THE GREEN LIGHT DISTRICT

The apostle Paul lived in the ***green light district*** of the Gospel.

He didn't need signs in the heavens to convince him to obey the Scriptures.

When Jesus said, "Go!" that was enough.

But he still needed the Holy Spirit to show him what was at the forefront of the Father's mind concerning mission.

239

Following the Command, Obeying the Voice

Paul was trying to obey what was on the pages of Scripture because he lived carrying the commandment *to go into all the world!* (See Matthew 28:19.) The old adage comes into play here; it's easier to steer the car when it's moving than when it's standing still.

Paul's commitment to the lifestyle of *going* put him in the place to hear the specific directions God had for him in that season. It was the Holy Spirit who was trying to keep him from going to certain places in wrong seasons.

THE PURPOSE OF REVELATION

Revelation is not poured out to make us smarter.

Insight is a wonderful benefit of this encounter, but our intelligence is not God's primary concern. His focus in revelation is our *personal transformation*.

241

LED TO A GOD-ENCOUNTER

Revelation leads to a God-encounter, and that encounter forever changes us.

The encounters can be stunning experiences or the simple moments of being immersed in His peace; but they are markers along the journey of, *"Thy kingdom come...."*

242

**Without a God-encounter,
revelation makes us proud.**

243

Revelation comes to enlarge the playing field of our faith.

244

THE BIRTHPLACE OF RELIGION

Insight without faith being released to have the truth realized through experience keeps truth unproven—only theory.

It is the birthplace of religion.

245

MORE THAN THEOLOGY

When God shows us that He wants people well, it is not to give us a theology on healing. It is so we will release our faith into the very area in which He's given us insight that we might experience the fruit of revelation—in this case, to heal people!

246

THE GREATER ANOINTING

Revelation means "to lift the veil" or "remove the cover."

Revelation gives us access to the *realms of greater anointing available* to us to make that truth a personal experience and lifestyle.

247

**The greater the truth,
the greater the anointing
needed to demonstrate
that truth to the world.**

248

Anointing must be pursued, not assumed. The measure of anointing that we carry reveals the measure of revelation we actually live in.

249

Unveiled to Children

"At that time Jesus answered and said, 'I thank You, Father, Lord of heaven and earth, that You have hidden these things from the wise and prudent and have revealed them to babes.'"
—Matthew 11:25

Can it be true that children are more open to revelation than adults? We tend to think that the weightier concepts are reserved for the mature. In part, that is true. But the really mature, from God's perspective, are those with a child's heart.

One of the greatest joys in life is hearing from God. There is no downside.

251

QUALIFIED TO HEAR

Simplicity and humility of heart helps qualify a person to hear from God, while the desire to be profound is a wasted desire.

252

What many discover after years of teaching is that the word that is simple is often the most profound.

253

"If anyone wills to do His will, he shall know concerning the doctrine, whether it is from God or whether I speak on My own authority."
—John 7:17

Clarity comes to the one willing to do the will of God.

254

The willingness to obey attracts revelation because God is the ultimate steward, investing His treasures into fertile ground—the surrendered heart.

"I call to remembrance my song in the night; I will meditate within my heart, and my spirit makes diligent search."
—Psalm 77:6

Biblical meditation is a diligent search.

Whereas religious cults teach people to empty their minds as the means of meditation, the Bible teaches us to fill our minds with God's Word.

256

THE EXPRESSION OF BIBLICAL MEDITATION

Meditation has a quiet heart and a "directed" mind.

Mulling a word over in our heart, with a pursuit that springs from the inquisitive child's heart, is meditation.

257

Living by faith in my present assignment makes me ready for more.

258

"He answered and said to them,
'Because it has been given to
you to know the mysteries of
the kingdom of heaven....'"
—MATTHEW 13:11

Revelation comes to the one expressing faith! Live with the understanding that God has already willed to give you His mysteries, and ask accordingly.

Then thank Him in advance.

259

Acquire an Understanding Heart

This sort of heart has the foundations in place for something to be constructed upon it.

These are the basic concepts of the King and His Kingdom.

Proper foundations attract the builder (revelator) to come and add to those foundations.

"But knowledge is easy to one
who has understanding."
—Proverbs 14:6 NASB

God wisely stewards fresh insight to those who have the basic principles in place.

When fresh insights come, the understanding heart has a "slot to put it in."

It is not lost as seed spilled on the ground.

261

Give God Your Nights

I try to end each day with my heart's affection stirred up and directed to the Holy Spirit.

What an amazing way to go to sleep.

262

"I sleep, but my heart is awake."
—Song of Solomon 5:2

God loves to visit us in the night and give us instruction that we would have a hard time receiving during the day.

263

The desire to give God our night season flows naturally from the child's heart that knows revelation cannot be earned.

264

Freely Give What You Have Received

Never underestimate what hungry people can "pull" from you while you minister the Word. Being in a place of continual giving is a sure way of getting more.

265

What God Put Inside of Us

When we're in "over our heads" in a ministry situation, we find out what God has been putting into us during the night. He draws out of the deep places in our hearts things that are not yet a part of our conscious thought processes.

266

"No longer do I call you servants, for a servant does not know what his master is doing; but I have called you friends, for all things that I heard from My Father I have made known to you."
—JOHN 15:15

Jesus makes *all things* known to His friends.

267

What's for You...and What's for Everyone Else

When God speaks, be accustomed to hearing more than you can share with others.

Listen as He speaks, but speak only what He gives you freedom to speak about.

Some things are revealed only because we're friends, and are not to be shared with others.

268

"Truly, truly, I say to you, we speak of what we know and testify of what we have seen, and you do not accept our testimony. If I told you earthly things and you do not believe, how will you believe if I tell you heavenly things?"
—JOHN 3:11-12 NASB

"*We*" refers to the Father, the Son, and the Holy Spirit.

It is *not* a reference to Jesus and His disciples or even Jesus and the angels.

269

Jesus said what He heard His Father say. The Spirit of God was upon Him, and made it possible for Him to succeed in hearing and seeing His Father clearly.

God has a testimony and is trying to pass on His story to anyone who would listen.

Because it's our responsibility to "loose here what is loosed in heaven" (see Matt. 16:19), we need to have a revelation of Heaven along with the heart to hear His testimony.

While it's true that God does not give His glory to another, we're not another—we are members of His Body.

272

CARRYING HIS WEIGHT

The ability to carry more has to do with both character and faith.

Character enables us to receive glorious promises of destiny without taking the glory to ourselves.

And greater faith responds to the declarations with the great courage needed for fulfillment.

New Realms of Revelation

The Holy Spirit was given to prepare the disciples for revelation at a whole new level.

He would take them where Jesus couldn't.

Perhaps this is part of the reason Jesus said,

"It is to your advantage that I go...."

274

The indwelling Holy Spirit enables us to bear more of the revelation of Jesus than was possible for the original twelve disciples.

275

It's Still Called Good News

The warnings of difficulties are necessary as they help us keep our priorities straight.

But it's the Father's good pleasure to give us the mysteries of the Kingdom.

And there's no pleasure in speaking of the death and destruction of the unrighteous (see Ezek. 33:11).

It's still called the *good news* for a reason.

276

"He will glorify Me, for He will take of Mine and will disclose it to you."
—JOHN 16:14 NASB

The Holy Spirit was given the task of not simply revealing all that Jesus possesses, but to actually "disclose" it to us. Disclose means to *declare!*

277

All belongs to the Father—the Father gives everything to the Son—the Son gives everything to us through the Holy Spirit who transfers the resources of Heaven into our account through His declaration.

278

Every declared promise is a transfer of heavenly resources that enable us to fulfill the purpose of our commission.

Hearing God is so vital because He transfers Jesus' inheritance into our accounts every time He speaks.

280

UNDERSTANDING, EXPERIENCE, INHERITANCE

One of the Holy Spirit's primary functions is to discover what lies in the depths of God's heart for us. He leads us into an understanding by experience to help us realize our inheritance.

281

"Now we have received, not the spirit of the world, but the [Holy] Spirit who is from God, so that we may know and understand the [wonderful] things freely given to us by God."
—1 Corinthians 2:12 AMP

This inheritance is freely given to us; it is the Holy Spirit who brings us into that *land of promise* that we might correctly navigate our way through life realizing the height, depth, length, and width of God's extravagant love for us. He unveils what is ours.

282

THE LIVING WORD

The Holy Spirit is also the one who makes the Scriptures come alive; it is the *living* Word. Learning to recognize His presence, His ways, and His language will help us to succeed in our impossible assignment.

Part Eight

Celebrating the Living Word

It's difficult to get the same fruit as the early church when we value a book they didn't have more than the Holy Spirit they did have.

283

HEARING THE SPEAKING GOD

God spoke and the worlds were made.

His Word creates.

The ability to hear God, especially from His Word, is a mandatory skill if we are to enter divine purpose and true creative expression.

284

The Prerequisite of a Yielded Heart

A yielded heart is impressionable as it studies Scripture and receives God's impressions (fingerprints) easily. Within that sort of tender soil, the Lord plants the seeds of Kingdom perspective that grow into global transformation.

ULTIMATE ANSWER BOOK

The insights and empowering nature of Scripture provide solutions applicable to every society and culture.

Hearing God is so vital because He transfers Jesus' inheritance into our accounts every time He speaks.

286

FROM STUDY TO EXPERIENCE

The study of Scriptures must take us beyond the historical setting, beyond language studies in the Hebrew and Greek, and at times beyond the context and intent of the human authors of Scripture.

It's time to hear from God afresh—that His Word would once again become the living Word in our experience.

CONSISTENT WITH THE WORD

I believe the Bible to be the Word of God, inerrant, fully inspired by the Holy Spirit. It is without equal, not to be added to nor subtracted from. Not only did God inspire the writers, He inspired those who selected which respective writings should be included to make up the full 66 books of the Bible. I do not believe there will be any new revelation that has the same authoritative weight as Scripture. It alone stands as judge of all other wisdom, be it the wisdom of man or an insight or book purported to be revealed directly from God or given by an angel.

God is still speaking, but everything we hear must be consistent with what He has spoken to us in His Word.

288

The Presence and the Scripture

Being unaware of God's presence has cost us dearly, especially as we approach Scripture.

King David, who authored and sang songs of His love for God's Word, "set" the Lord before himself daily.

He purposed to be regularly conscious of God's nearness and lived from that mindset.

289

SANCTIFIED IMAGINATION

The sanctified imagination is a tool in God's hand that enables us to tap into true reality.

My approach is this—I can't imagine a place where He isn't, so I might as well imagine Him with me. This is not vain imagination. Rather, it's vain to imagine otherwise.

290

Living by Principle or by Presence?

There is a style of Scripture reading that is mainly concerned with finding and applying principles rather than enjoying His presence. This is good but limited. Kingdom principles are real and powerful. They can be taught to anyone. When they are applied to life, they bring forth fruit for the King. Even unbelievers will experience blessing when they live by His principles.

I am not knocking the principles. The transformation of cities and nations depends on the receptivity of Kingdom principles. However, this is not the core of the Christian's experience with the Bible. Rather, more often than not we should read to have a God-encounter.

291

To value the Scriptures above the Holy Spirit is idolatry. It is not Father, Son, and Holy Bible; it's the Holy Spirit.

292

The Bible reveals God but is itself not God. It does not contain Him. God is bigger than His book.

293

READING SCRIPTURE UNDER THE HOLY SPIRIT'S INFLUENCE

We are reliant on the Holy Spirit to reveal what is contained on the pages of Scripture, because without Him it is a closed book. Such dependency on the Holy Spirit must be more than a token prayer asking for guidance before a Bible study. It is a relationship with the third person of the Trinity that is continuous, ongoing, and affects every single aspect of life.

294

REVEALED TO THE HUNGRY

Holy Spirit is the wind that blows in uncertain directions, from unknown places (see John 3:8). He is the power of Heaven and cannot be controlled but must be yielded to.

He eagerly reveals His mysteries to all who are hungry—truly hungry.

295

RE-EMPHASIZING HOLY SPIRIT

The Holy Spirit is de-emphasized and almost removed from many Christians' daily approach to life and the Word. The fear of becoming like some mindless fanatic has kept many a Christian from interacting with their greatest treasure in this life—the Holy Spirit.

We are heirs of God, and the Holy Spirit is the down payment of our inheritance (see Eph. 1:13-14).

296

Some teach that we shouldn't talk much about the Spirit as the Holy Spirit doesn't speak of Himself. However, both the Father and Son have a lot to say about Him. It is wise to listen to them.

God is to be praised, adored, boasted in, and interacted with—and the Holy Spirit is God.

297

A FRESH APPROACH TO SCRIPTURE

The approach of many believers to Scripture is inconsistent with the Spirit who inspired those sacred writings. Much of what we have a heart to accomplish cannot be done without reexamining our relationship with God through His Word.

298

A New View

We have gone as far as we can go with what we presently know.

Not only are we in need of the Spirit of God to teach us, we are in need of a different view of the Bible.

299

THE POWER OF HIS WORD

The Word of God is living and active.

It contains divine energy, always moving and accomplishing His purposes.

It is the surgeon's knife that cuts in order to heal.

It is balm that brings comfort and healing.

300

Living Words

The Word of God is multidimensional and unfolding in nature.

When Isaiah spoke a word, it applied to the people he spoke to—his contemporaries.

Yet because it is alive, much of what he said then has its ultimate fulfillment in another day and time. Living words do that.

TRUTH IN SEASON

God said we were to choose whom we would serve, yet Jesus said He chose us; we didn't choose Him. We are predestined from before the foundation of the world, yet are told that *whosoever will* may come. Jesus said we had to sell all to follow Him, yet He instructs the wealthy to be rich in good works.

The Holy Spirit knows what truth to breathe on according to the particular season of our life.

302

THE MULTIDIMENSIONAL NATURE OF TRUTH

Truth is multidimensional. Some truths are superior to others.

Lesser truths are often the foundation of greater truths.

"I no longer call you servants, but friends" (see John 15:15).

Friendship with God is built on the foundation of first being a servant.

Truth is progressive in nature—line upon line, precept on precept.

303

OVERPOWERED BY LOVE

The primary message of the Old Testament is to reveal the power of sin.

For that reason when a person touched a leper, they became unclean.

Sin is overpowering. Flee from it!

The primary message of the New Testament is the power of God's love.

So when Jesus touched a leper, the leper became clean.

"Love covers a multitude of sin."

Both messages are true. One is greater. Love is overpowering!

304

New Rules for a New Level

The desire for static rules is our basic preference for the law.

Preset boundaries are what keep us obedience focused instead of relationship focused.

One is set on memorized rules and regulations.

The other is entirely set on God's voice and presence and the rules and regulations sit at a different level.

305

OBEDIENCE OUT OF LOVE

When the woman caught in adultery was brought before Jesus, He decided to enforce His own rules and law in a way contrary to what the law demanded. And Jesus only did what He saw the Father doing.

Obedience will always be important for us.

But obedience out of love looks a lot different from obedience because of rules.

306

Present Truth

To say the Scripture changes is an uncomfortable concept. It doesn't change in the sense that it passes away or contradicts itself, but it does change in the same way a wineskin expands to reflect the ever-increasing move of the Spirit of God.

In Deuteronomy 23:1, the Lord commands that an emasculated man *"shall not enter the assembly of the Lord."* Yet in Isaiah 56:3-5, the eunuch who holds fast to the covenant will be given an everlasting name which will not be cut off.

Finally, in Acts 8 Phillip converts a eunuch who becomes the very first evangelist to Ethiopia.

Peter called this sort of movement "present truth."

307

KNOWING THE AUTHOR

The problem is not our tendency to incorrectly interpret Scripture; it's that after 2,000 years with the Holy Spirit being on the earth and in us, we still don't know Him! The rule is not the answer.

Repentance for ignoring the third person of the Trinity is the beginning of the much-needed solution.

That alone can take us into realms in God that have previously been thought impossible for an entire generation to experience.

308

Doctrine must be a wineskin kept elastic by the oil of the Spirit. If it is rigid and unmoving, it will not yield to God's habit of opening up more of His Word to us.

309

ENHANCING WHAT WE THINK WE KNOW

God loves to add to our knowledge things we think we already understand.

Too much rigidity bursts our doctrinal wineskins under the weight of ongoing revelation.

The end result is the churchs become irrelevant and powerless to the world around them.

310

DON'T BUILD A MONUMENT

It is easy to prefer a particular theological slant, build a monument around it, and become deaf or adversarial to its important counterpoint.

For example, I am much more Armenian in background than I am Calvinist. Yet some of my dearest friends are Calvinists. I love to hear the Holy Spirit work through them, because there is freshness to what they teach. I become convinced of God's sovereignty and leave that meeting with a conviction that "God chose me; I didn't choose Him!" Conversely, when I sit in a meeting where the opposite point is stressed, I also leave with conviction—that of freewill, the power of our choice, my responsibility as a delegated one on this planet, and that the outcome of His purposes depends upon the faithfulness of God's people.

Which is true? Both are.

311

The Holy Spirit has to be free to speak to us about the things that are on His heart, especially those things to which we have a natural resistance.

312

DON'T TRADE TRUTH FOR CONVENIENCE OR COMFORT

We must be open to truth when it has a biblical basis and is accompanied by the breath of God making it come alive for a specific purpose. The error is building a theological monument around a particular point of view that conveniently excludes certain portions of Scripture to help us feel secure in a doctrinal bent.

313

I am concerned with our tendency to gather around doctrines instead of around spiritual fathers. The former builds denominations, while the latter creates movements.

314

Spirit-Expanded Doctrine

Even our most valued doctrines can be expanded under the inspiration of the Holy Spirit. Usually, it's not the expansion that we have the most difficulty with. It is when He begins to speak about what is, at first glance, a contradiction to what we have learned.

315

WILLING TO EMBRACE THE CONTRADICTION

The desire for rigid doctrine is in direct proportion to our inability to actually hear His voice.

It's essential to be able to recognize His voice so we can embrace His revelation, even when it contradicts our traditional upbringing.

316

MAINTAINING A CHILDLIKE HEART

Becoming an expert in any area of Scripture is the very thing that often closes us off from learning the new things that God is opening up in His Word.

It's the childlike heart that attracts revelation from God (see Matt. 11:25).

317

I must come to that which I understand with a childlike heart because what I know can keep me from what I need to know if I don't remain a novice.

318

PERFECT THEOLOGY

Jesus Christ is perfect theology.

He is the *"exact representation of His nature"* (Heb. 1:3 NASB), the ultimate portrayal of the Father.

Questions that exist about God's nature in the Old Testament were clarified in the New Testament.

319

"Till we all come to the unity of the faith and of the knowledge of the Son of God, to a perfect man, to the measure of the stature of the fullness of Christ."
—EPHESIANS 4:13

Coming into maturity is the result of gaining the *knowledge of the Son of God.*

This revelation will completely change the church as we know it today, because as we see Him we become like Him.

This will enable us to accurately represent Jesus.

320

A Disciple of Jesus (Not Job)

When I teach about God's absolute desire and provision to heal, I am asked, "What about Job?"

I respond, "I'm not a disciple of Job; I'm a disciple of Jesus."

321

JESUS ANSWERS THE QUESTION

Job's life helped create the awareness for the need of a savior.

Job is the question. Jesus is the answer.

If our study of Job (and other Old Testament issues) doesn't lead us to Jesus as the answer, it reveals we never really understood the question.

322

Jesus Is the Standard

The types and symbols of the Old Testament do not override the clear manifestation of God through Jesus in the New Testament. Any understanding we have about the nature of God that can't be seen in the person of Jesus must be questioned.

323

Jesus messed up every funeral He attended, including His own.

324

No Theology for Bad Experiences

When the disciples asked Him about their failed attempt to bring deliverance to a child, He gave them instructions on how to get their breakthrough. He said it would come through *prayer and fasting* (see Mark 9:29).

It's time to respond to His counsel and discover for ourselves how to get the breakthrough that appears to be so elusive. He manifested the will of God. And we must not change it to fit our experience. It is time to manifest the will of God again.

325

HEARING REFINED THROUGH FAILURE

It is obvious and easy to assert that those who try to hear God from the pages of Scripture will not always hear clearly. Some of us will make huge mistakes and claim to have heard from God when it wasn't Him at all.

Yet to succeed, one must be willing to fail.

326

The area of our greatest risk, though we have previously failed, can become our greatest area of authority if we won't give up.

327

WHAT COUNTERFEITS TELL US

Counterfeiters don't make fake pennies; it's not worth the effort.

I know that if the enemy works hard to create a counterfeit, the original must have great value.

Only things of eternal consequence are worth the devil's attention.

328

Christianity was never to be known by its disciplines. It's to be known by its passion.

329

Demons are attracted to religiously sanitized environments where there is no power.

330

We Need Both: Scripture and Power

Both the Scriptures and the power of God are essential!

There is *no* justification for lack in either area.

The stream of theological accuracy and the stream of experiential Christianity will merge as we learn to give honor to one another in our pursuit of a full demonstration of the Gospel.

331

DEFINING BIBLICAL MEDITATION

Biblical meditation is a completely different animal than what is encouraged in the New Age culture. Theirs is a counterfeit because it encourages us to empty our minds, making them vulnerable to any *angel of light* to enter and eventually control.

Unfortunately, there are many evil spirits looking for a vacancy.

332

DESPERATION FOR TRUTH

Our desperation for truth makes us available for things that others seem to continually miss. Keeping a pure heart makes the journey to God's Word a journey where nothing is impossible.

333

WHAT YOU CARRY TO THE WATERING HOLE

If I come to God's Word with evangelism on my mind, it seems that evangelism is on every page of my Bible. All the stories reaffirm my understanding of God's heart for people, but open up new Scriptures that I never previously considered to be evangelistic. The same is true of finances. If I come to God's Word with money on my mind, it appears that the whole Bible teaches about stewardship.

This principle is true of most any subject you could mention. What you carry to this watering hole will determine much of what you see and reproduce.

Part Nine

Redesigning Our World

The Holy Spirit is imprisoned in the bodies of unbelieving believers.

334

"Death and life are in the power of the tongue."
—PROVERBS 18:21

With our speech we design and alter our environment.

Realities are created that didn't exist a moment earlier through simple proclamations.

With this tool we can build up or tear down, edify or discourage, give life or destroy it. The declared word has the capacity to resource earth with Heaven's resources.

335

The Responsibility of Reformers

As reformers we must first pay attention to what we say, realizing that we are actually building the world we have to live in. We have the ability to speak *from* God, revealing His world and His ways.

336

"ALL THINGS" HAVE BEEN PROVIDED!

"Therefore let no one boast in men.
For all things are yours."
—1 CORINTHIANS 3:21

The transfer of "all things," our inheritance, begs this question, "Why would God give us all things?" Because *all things* will be necessary for us to fulfill the commission that God has given us. Our assignment from God will require the use of "all things" to be under our supervision to accomplish His purposes on earth.

337

Supernatural Gift of Encouragement

One of the essential tools necessary to redefine the nature of the world around us is the gift of *encouragement.* This profound instrument has all of Heaven's attention. When angels perceive its use, they know their assignment has been released.

It is more than a natural use of words to make someone feel good about themselves or their circumstances; it is supernatural in nature and partners with Heaven to bring forth Heaven's response.

338

Declarations That Release "Kingdom Come"

In the same way the Holy Spirit transfers our inheritance to us through the declaration, so we release heavenly realms through our speech.

In God's economy, without declaration there is no creation (see Ps. 33:6).

Deliberate declarations in line with the covenantal promises of God are essential for the transformation of the kingdoms of this world.

339

CHANGING THE IMAGE OF CHRISTIANITY

The average unbeliever is not accustomed to Christians having something nice to say about them. Christianity is known more for what we don't like than for what we do like.

In spite of our shortcomings, we have been given this wonderful gift to distinguish us from the rest—the grace to encourage. When we encourage, it is more than a *feel-good moment;* it actually releases the favor of God.

340

ALL THE ANSWERS ARE IN HIS DOMINION

Contained in the realm of the Kingdom of God are all the answers to life's problems.

It doesn't matter if it's the crisis with the ozone layer, frustration in dealing with contentious neighbors, or a problem with a failing marriage or business; the realm of the King's dominion has the answer. That realm of dominion is the realm of the Holy Spirit manifesting the lordship of Jesus Christ, which is first realized in our hearts.

341

"The kingdom of God is within you."
—Luke 17:21

All the Kingdom issues are heart issues. Properly dealing with attitudes, ambitions, and agendas is key to enjoying the reign of God displayed in our lives.

Our relationship with the Holy Spirit is foundational to the breakthroughs that we all want to see.

342

"To you it has been granted to know the mysteries of the kingdom."
—LUKE 8:10 NASB

The secrets of God are our inheritance.

We have access to this reality for the sake of those around us.

The wonderful things that are to become manifest to the world are to flow from us.

God intended that His expression to the world spring from *within His people.*

343

"Keep your heart with all diligence,
for out of it spring the issues of life."
—Proverbs 4:23

What is going on inside of us affects what goes on around us. This principle affects health, relationships, success in our occupation, and our gifts and ministries.

All things flow from the heart.

Sleeping in the Storm

In Mark chapter 4, Jesus was in a life-threatening storm with the disciples. To their surprise, He was asleep.

I've heard people say He slept because He was exhausted.

I'd like to suggest that He slept because the world He was *living in* had no storms.

345

We have authority over any storm we can sleep in, as we can only give away what we've received.

346

CHANGE IN YOUR INTERNAL WORLD

Sometimes we focus on merely changing our words, knowing that they carry creative force. Still it's out of the heart that the mouth speaks. Changing the external without dealing with the heart is the way of religion.

The push for miracles is the same. Trying to obtain a measure of Kingdom expression on the outside that is not manifest on the inside is the sign that the cruel taskmaster of religion is present. In the command to do the miraculous we find the key, *"Freely you have received, freely give"* (Matt. 10:8).

We can give away *kingdom in the measure* we experience the *King's dominion* within us.

347

What reigns on the inside rains on the outside.

As it was with Peter's shadow, whatever overshadows me will be released through my shadow.

348

THE BARRIER TO CREATIVITY

The soul that is bound by worry, jealousy, anger, resentment, and the like is incapable of creativity on a consistent basis. It's impossible to thrive in that divine privilege because we are functioning separately from our design.

Full potential is only found by carrying what God gave us to carry—"*my burden is light*" (Matt. 11:30).

349

Displaying the Wisdom of God

We are to display the wisdom of God to be seen by all those in positions of power—including the principalities and powers in heavenly places. The creative expression that comes through wisdom is a reminder to all that exists that this company of believers is commissioned to bring heavenly answers to earthly problems. This will turn heads from the inferior wisdom of this world to the divine wisdom that answers the cry of the human heart.

350

Our assignment is to live as though nothing were impossible.

The command to disciple nations is not figurative. It was a literal command that has the backing of Heaven for those who embrace the assignment.

351

Occupy and Advance!

Regardless of how and when you believe we are going to be taken to Heaven, we must rid ourselves of the idea that Jesus is coming to *rescue* His Church. That lie has dislocated many generations of revolutionaries from their purpose in the same way a joint is pulled out of place.

It has put the Church into a defensive posture of occupation to protect what we have instead of positioning ourselves for the purpose of increase. The strategy of occupation for the purpose of advancement and increase is an absolute Kingdom principle.

Part Ten

Pulling Tomorrow into Today

We own in the present what is not yet.

352

SHAPING OUR WORLD

Our role in shaping the world around us through creative expression is never more at the forefront than when we joyfully learn to pull tomorrow into today. God trains us for this role whenever He speaks to us, for in doing so He is working to awaken and establish our affections for His Kingdom.

A people whose hearts are anchored in His world are best qualified to serve in this one.

353

When His World Influences Our World

God establishes His eternal purpose in us whenever He speaks. His Word comes from eternity into time, giving us a track to ride on. It connects us with eternity, causing us to impact our world through the influence of His world.

354

The believer's inheritance is beyond human comprehension. To put the richness of that gift into the eternal future is to sell short the power of the Cross in the present.

God gave us a gift beyond comprehension because we have an assignment beyond reason.

Jesus gave us *all things* because we would need *all things* to fulfill our call. He intends to fill the earth with His glory, and His glorious Bride will play a role.

356

THE DEMAND OF MIRACLES

Seeing God display His wonders has a price tag—we can no longer live (think and act) the same way we did before.

Miracles display God's dominion with a clarity that is seldom seen in the rest of life.

To see and not change is to bring judgment upon ourselves.

357

A Glimpse of Tomorrow...Today

If God lets you see future promises, it's because He's hoping they will hook you and cause you to hunger for those things.

It is through a desperate heart that you are able to bring the fulfillment of those promises into your day.

358

ACCELERATION THROUGH DESPERATION

All of the promises God reveals to us will be realized in time, but the acceleration of events is largely determined by the desperation of His people. Our passion for the Lord and His promises speeds up the process of growth and development, making us qualified for the stewardship of those events sooner than had been planned.

359

Don't Sweep His Promises Under the Millennium Rug

We have a bad habit of taking most of the good promises of the Bible and sweeping them under the mysterious rug we call "the millennium." It is a great inconsistency to say the last days began with the day of Pentecost with Acts 2, and then take the wonderful promises of the prophets about the last days and say they refer to the millennium.

A SUMMONS

If it's true that the promises of restored cities and healed nations are actually millennium promises...and if the promise of God's glory being manifest all over the earth is far off into the future...and if in fact the people of God will not reach a place of true maturity, living like one mature man—then I must ask these questions:

Is there anyone hungry enough for what He has shown us in the Scriptures that we will pull into our day something that is reserved for another?

Is there anyone willing to lay themselves down to bring more of God's promises across another great divide?

Or how about the promise that says everyone will know the Lord? (See Jeremiah 31:34.)

Isn't that one worth pursuing for our cities?

361

THE CURSED FIG TREE'S CHALLENGE

There's a message for us in the cursed fig tree. Jesus cursed it for not bearing fruit *out of season.* It died immediately. Was He unreasonable? Did He lose His temper? Or was He showing us something about His expectations for our lives that we'd just as soon ignore?

Jesus has the right to expect the fruit of the impossible from those He has created for the impossible.

QUALIFIED FOR THE IMPOSSIBLE

The Spirit of the resurrected Christ living in me has disqualified me from the mundane and ordinary. I am qualified for the impossible, because I'm a believing believer.

Faith qualifies me for the impossible.

363

Moving the Resources of Heaven

God doesn't reveal coming events to make us strategists. He shows us the future to make us dissatisfied because hungry people move the resources of Heaven like no one else possibly could.

364

Shaped by Contending Prayer

Contending shapes us and makes us capable of carrying more than we've ever been able before, and it opens up for us areas of anointing in ministry that were previously out of reach.

OUR TIME TO RUN

We have been given the right to surpass the accomplishments of previous generations using creativity through wisdom to solve the issues facing us. Their ceiling is our floor.

This is our time to run.

About Bill Johnson

Bill Johnson is a fifth-generation pastor with a rich heritage in the Holy Spirit. Together Bill and his wife serve a growing number of churches that have partnered for revival. This leadership network has crossed denominational lines, building relationships that enable church leaders to walk successfully in both purity and power. Bill and his wife, Beni, are the senior leaders of Bethel Church, Redding, California. All three of their children and spouses are involved in full-time ministry. They also have nine wonderful grandchildren.

Looking for more from

BILL JOHNSON AND BETHEL CHURCH?

Purchase additional resources—CDs, DVDs, digital downloads, music—from Bill Johnson and the Bethel team at the **online Bethel store.**

Visit www.bjm.org for more information on Bill Johnson, to view his speaking itinerary, or to look into additional teaching resources.

To order Bethel Church resources, visit http://store.ibethel.org

Subscribe to Bethel.TV to access the latest sermons, worship sets, and conferences from Bethel Church. To subscribe, visit www.bethel.tv

Become part of a Supernatural Culture that is transforming the world and *apply* for the Bethel School of Supernatural Ministry

For more information, visit bssm.net